The
Sanford Meisner
Approach

AN ACTOR'S WORKBOOK

The
Sanford Meisner
Approach

AN ACTOR'S WORKBOOK

Larry Silverberg

A Career Development Book

SK

A Smith and Kraus Book

A Smith and Kraus Book
Published by Smith and Kraus, Inc.
177 Lyme Road, Hanover, NH 03755
www.smithandkraus.com

Manufactured in the United States of America

First Edition: November 1994
6 5 4 3 2 1

Library of Congress Cataloging-in-Publication Data

Silverberg, Larry, 1959 -
    The Sanford Meisner approach : an actors workbook / by Larry Silverberg.
        p. cm. -- (A career development book)
    ISBN-10 1-880399-77-6 ISBN-13: 978-1-880399-77-4 : $14.95
    1. Acting. 2. Meisner, Sanford. I. Title. II. Series.
    PN2061.S55   1994
    792'.028--dc20   94-38079
                                                              CIP

For Jill

Biography

LARRY SILVERBERG, author of the four-volume series *The Sanford Meisner Approach: An Actor's Workbook,* the two-volume series *The Actor's Guide to Qualified Acting Coaches,* and *Loving to Audition,* is a graduate of the Neighborhood Playhouse School of Theatre where he studied with master acting teacher Sanford Meisner. Since then he has worked professionally as an actor and director across the United States and in Canada. Most recently, Larry received the Seattle Critic's Association Stellar Acting Award for his portrayal of Teach in the Belltown Theatre Center production of David Mamet's *American Buffalo.*

Larry also teaches his professional intensive: the Meisner Actor's Training Program in New York City, and he has taught master classes in the Meisner work at universities, high school, and acting studios in many parts of the world. If you are interested in studying with Larry or having him teach his visiting workshops at your school, please contact him by telephone at (212) 462-3005 or write to him care of Smith and Kraus Publishers, PO Box 127, Lyme, NH 03768. Read more about Larry or contact him via his website address at www.actorscraft.com.

Contents

Acknowledgments

Part I

First, thank you to my three greatest partners and wisest teachers, my wife Jill and our children Sarah and Aaron. You make it all worth it. All of it!

To Sanford Meisner, thank you Sandy for all the continually unfolding miracles that your work and working with you have made possible in my life. And for the moments of beauty given to all of us by the work of all your extraordinary students.

To my friend, Horton Foote, has been a most generous ally in every aspect of my life. He has gone to great lengths to assist me in some very difficult times, and he was an enthusiastic partner in helping me make this book a reality. I have learned so much about what is of most importance in life, about simplicity, compassion, and forgiveness, from Horton. I am deeply grateful to him. Thank you Horton!

To Sheila and Bernie Silverberg (Mom and Dad!) and all of my family in Florida, and to Helen and Skip Rooney, thank you all for your unwavering support. For her own very special and unceasing presence in my life and work, I am forever grateful to my Grandma Ethel, (Thanks Grandma!) Thank you, my dear, loving, Edith Stein, Mother Michael and all of the nuns at St. Joseph's Carmelite Monastery in Seattle, WA.

Thanks to my oldest and greatest friend (we go back to third grade together!), Dick Kowal, who is always cheering me on and giving me good, solid advice when I'm getting carried away. If we were older and British, Dick and I would have been the Beatles.

I also want to thank my wonderful acting teacher, Suzanne Shepherd, and all of my teachers at the Neighborhood Playhouse. My deep appreciation to James Price for his generosity and support through the years. Thanks also to Harold Baldridge, Jim Carville, Connie Clausen, Robbie Burns, Richard Janaro, Jorge Guerra, Ellen Davis and all of my friends at the New World School of the Arts in Miami. Much appreciation to Dannul and Tinka Dailey, Robin Smith and George Lewis here in Seattle and to the illuminating Arthur Giron.

Thank you to my publishers, Marisa Smith and the wonderfully calm Eric Kraus, and to all of the great staff at Smith and Kraus.

There certainly would be no book were it not for the deeply committed and courageous students I have worked with all around the country. I am grateful to all of you! I especially thank my students who are struggling to bring to life their company Tenderfoote at my theater, the Belltown Theatre Center here in Seattle, Washington.

Part II
Stewart Stern

My immediate impulse, whenever I have to write something—especially something important—is to call Stewart Stern to rescue me. And he has! I have sat with Stewart countless times, howling out all of my thoughts and feelings in the most inarticulate way. Then, very quietly, Stewart will turn to me and ask, "Is this what you are saying?" And, as if he were a secret visitor in my dreams, out of his mouth come the most vivid images and sounds, a heightened poetic life expressing everything that my heart had been whispering to me in my most private moments. So here I am again, wishing desperately that I could run to Stewart and ask him to help me express, in words, how much he means to me and how deep an impact he has had on my life!

Although Stewart is mostly known as one of the greatest screenwriters of our time and for the extraordinary films he helped create (*Rebel without a Cause, Rachel Rachel, Sybil, The Ugly American, Summer Wishes Winter Dreams,* and others), I want you to know about some of his other gifts.

Stewart is the most interested person who ever walked this planet. He is absolutely and in every moment fascinated. By everyone and everything!

And though he has a wealth of wisdom about life and reality, his face is always beaming with that joyful glow of the excited beginner who is discovering for the first time.

As he has in my life, I have watched, day after day, Stewart passionately making a difference in so many peoples' lives. His concern and generosity are huge, his heart even bigger. He thrives on making a difference. He thrives on embracing you, wherever you're at. And when you have been with Stewart, you leave feeling bigger than when you came. I think Stewart's greatest medium as an artist is life—his canvas, the world, animals and other people around him. I have often left Stewart's house, after one of our three hours talks, feeling very much like a rare work of art that has been studied, admired, and loved.

As Jill and I have been building and growing a theatre here in Seattle, Stewart has been our most passionate advocate and advisor. He has spent endless hours thinking and consulting, planning and writing, visiting with students, seeking and getting funding, and bringing on board other people who have become vital allies. Stewart has been our greatest partner in attempting to create something wonderful and alive here.

So, thank you Stewart, thank you so much for all that you have given to me and for everything that you are!

Preface

American acting and the American training of actors has been greatly influenced by four actor-director-teachers: Lee Strasberg, Stella Adler, Robert Lewis and Sanford Meisner. Two of them, Strasberg and Adler, studied with Maria Ouspenskaya and Richard Boveslavsky—who had studied with and been directed by Stanislavsky. Later, Strasberg, Adler, Lewis and Meisner worked together at the Group Theatre where they further explored Stanislavsky's theories about acting and the training of actors.

Although this was their common root, they each interpreted Stanislavsky's ideas in their own way, combining his techniques with ideas of their own as they worked. Since then, these teachers have all trained many actors, directors, and teachers of acting, who have in turn trained another generation in the theater.

Sanford Meisner taught for many years at the Neighborhood Playhouse, where he directed and produced dozens of plays, including several of my own. For several years before he left the Playhouse, he would ask me to come and direct his students in one of my plays. He was greatly talented as an actor and director, and, of course, as a teacher. He has always had a great love for the theatre and for actors and was most generous in sharing his knowledge with his students and others. In his work at the Playhouse and in his private classes he has trained many of our most distinguished actors and directors, as well as many of our most successful acting teachers.

Which brings me to Larry Silverberg: a gifted actor and director and a most inspired teacher of acting. Larry first impressed me with a production of one of my plays which he directed in Florida. Since then, I have seen some of his work in his Seattle Theatre, (again on a play of mine), and I am continually impressed with his resourcefulness and his dedication to his art. Occasionally, I get discouraged about the direction our theater is taking today, but when someone surfaces with the vision, passion, and talent of Larry Silverberg, I am reassured.

Both Silverberg's debt to Meisner and his own perception and clarity are evident in these exercises. This book touches the heart of the Meisner Approach as I understand it.

Larry begins by emphasizing that, in the best of all possible worlds, one would study acting with a qualified teacher. However, when this is not possible, this book will prove invaluable. Indeed, it should be of great value to anyone interested in our present theatre and in the techniques of training actors.

—Horton Foote

Until one is committed, there is hesitancy, the chance to draw back, always ineffectiveness. Concerning all acts of initiative and creation there is one elementary truth the ignorance of which kills countless ideas and splendid plans: that the moment one definitely commits oneself then providence moves too.

All sorts of things occur to help one that would never otherwise have occurred. A whole stream of events issue from the decision, raising in one's favour all manner of unforeseen incidents and meetings and material assistance, which no man could have dreamed would have come his way.

Whatever you can do or dream you can begin it, boldness has genius, power and magic in it.

Begin it now.

—Goethe

Introduction

Welcome!

I have realized that my impulse to write this book comes from two facts, I say facts because I know them to be true.

1) Who you truly are is magnificent and totally unique.

2) The work I am going to share with you, the Sanford Meisner Approach, is miraculous.

Maybe you are beginning your studies as an actor and you are excited and passionate. You have strong feelings about people, life, the world around you and you are hungry to find the ways to use all of yourself to express those deep feelings, to make a tremendous difference through your acting.

Or, perhaps you are cautious, nervous even. You've always wanted to give acting a try and there's that little voice inside you, calling to you once more and with a greater urgency, "Go on, go on, what are you waiting for!" And you find yourself in the theater aisle of the bookstore with my book in your hands, reading the introduction to see if this is the one for you.

Maybe you have studied acting, a little here and a little there and you have noticed that there have been moments in your acting when something has "clicked" and afterwards you thought, "That is exactly where I want to be in my acting!" But you're not really sure what happened, how it happened or how to have it happen again. It all seems to be hit or miss. And you wish you had something solid, in terms of technique, that you could count on. Something from which to build on and to grow with.

Maybe you have acted some—in college or community theater or professionally—and you have been pushed to results so quickly and so often that you feel you have lost touch with your own creative center. You find that when you are really honest with yourself, you have to admit that acting just isn't that much fun for you anymore. And you long to re-connect with your heart in your work, with that joyous spark that got you into acting in the first place.

If you recognize yourself in any of those statements, you've come to the right place. Which brings me back to those two facts:

Who you truly are is magnificent and totally unique.

The work I am going to share with you, the Sanford Meisner Approach, is miraculous.

And I do not bring up miracles lightly. Let me tell you, when students have a moment in an acting exercise in which they suddenly experience themselves as so much greater and more powerful than they were aware of; more expressive and spontaneous, more deeply caring, concerned and interested than they ever thought possible; that they can be totally available and receptive to their partners as well as to their own passionate spirit; that they are courageous and ready to take risks, able to fight for what they know to be true and honest enough to say, "Yes, I am wrong", to be generous and forgiving and willing to ask for forgiveness—a moment from which their life will never be the same and from which they learn in a vital way that acting is about being fully alive, fully authentic; about being the complete expression of ones greater truth and that it is more joyous than they ever could have imagined, <u>NOW THAT'S MIRAC-</u> <u>ULOUS!</u>

And you know what? It is this kind of personal transformation that I have been privileged to witness in my classes countless times. It is the great leaping off place in one's pursuit of the craft of acting. And it is why as a professional actor and director these last fourteen years since graduating from the Neighborhood Playhouse, I also continually and ecstatically return to the classroom as acting coach, to share the brilliant process given to us by my teacher, the great acting teacher of our time, Sanford Meisner, "Sandy!"

And so, it is why I wrote this book. I'd be a liar if I told you that I thought there was another acting technique as effective as the Meisner work. Am I biased? ABSOLUTELY! And I didn't want to give you just one more interesting book to read, (although you may find this book vastly interesting) my aim was to give you a specific, <u>step-by-step</u> way of actually doing the foundation exercises of Sandy's approach. My hope is that this book will become deeply valuable to you as you discover and forge your own, very personal, approach to acting and to the theatre.

You may wonder if you can do these acting exercises. You may be asking yourself those old, nagging questions, "Do I have the ability, am I talented, can I make it?" Let's get this clear right now. You must leave all of that alone and put your energy into one thing, doing the work! You see, the rest is out of your control, so why bother with it? I am telling you that you do have the ability, but you know, a better question to ask yourself is, "Am I ready to be *unreasonable with myself?*"

Also, this book is not meant to replace your working with a good acting coach. (A good teacher will interact with you and create an environment that supports your growth as an actor in ways that are possible nowhere else.) What I intend this book to do, is to give you a great start; to strengthen you and prepare you so that your work with good teachers (acting coaches, directors and other actors...) will go very deep and will be very true. Also, your work here will help you to know who your real teachers are—and maybe protect you from the rest.

· · · · · · · ·

Everything I say to you in this book is the truth. I am speaking to you now as an actor, for all that I have available to me on stage is my own point of view, the truth as I know it, and I must hold on to it and fight for it with my life! There are many acting techniques and the ones that are valid will help you arrive at the one ultimate truth, your truth. The work we will do together will lead you to acting with a deep personal meaning, a wonderful simplicity (so rare in the theatre) and to a level of working where technique disappears and what remains is you in your acting.

You know, if someone in the audience leaves saying "That was a real Meisner actor," it would all have been a waste of time. When you give them the real thing, the audience will leave talking not so much about you but about their lives. They will run out and call their sister who they haven't talked with in ten years or hurry home to hug their daughter, they will move out of a terrible situation or confront their boss—they will be altered in some way—and they will come to you backstage and say "Thank you!"

How To Use This Book

This is a workbook. I will be giving you very specific things to do. You cannot do this work alone, you must work with an acting partner. Also, the most effective approach would be to have a group of at least three people so that when two partners are working, another person can become the "Observer."

Throughout the book, two people as the "Partners," will be taken through a series of acting exercises. Like building blocks, with each step we lay the groundwork for what is next and only the doing of each exercise will allow the possibility of what is to follow. A third person as the "Observer," will receive instructions on what to be looking for and how to simply interact with the partners who are doing the exercises. If you have more than three people in your group, rotate as the Observer so that everyone has this experience. You will find that there is a tremendous amount of learning that takes place when you are in the Observer role!

As partners or as a group, you can work through this process on your own or if you have an acting teacher that you trust and who would be excited to go through this workbook with you (to serve as the Observer,) that's fine too. Either way is OK.

• • • • • • • •

The book is divided into "Sessions" and I request that you do one Session a week. This is your "work meeting." (This will hold true until Session Eleven, at which time I will be giving you somewhat different instructions.) You will also be given homework to do between sessions. Part of this homework will require you to meet with a partner to practice the exercises a minimum of two times a week. (Of course, you could meet to practice daily, fantastic!) The other part will be personal work. I ask that you get a journal for the personal work and that you keep a running record of your experiences as you go through the Sessions. Bring this journal with you to all Sessions to take notes, to answer questions that I will ask you from time to time, and to do the structured journal work in the latter Sessions.

Together, we will build an exercise that, ultimately, contains all of the dramatic elements. As you do these exercises consistently, your acting skills will grow and strengthen. The key words here are *do* and *consistently.* Like the dancer at the bar or the pianist playing endless scales, learning the craft of acting does not happen in our talking about, thinking about, or reading about, which may all be very intellectually appealing but will remain in your head merely as concept or theory. As with any craft, true learning occurs only in the doing of it and with time.

• • • • • • • •

I promise you, that as you go through this work, you will have all kinds of responses to it. It may at one moment excite you and the next bore you. You may at times hate it with a passion and be totally perplexed and soon after find you are joyous in the work and it is all making sense. I ask that you allow yourself to have all that you are experiencing AND keep on working. Do not allow how you are feeling about it to get in the way of doing the work, know that everything you experience is appropriate and part of your own process. Also, I want you to know that this work happens very much in a two-steps-forward-then-four-steps-back—five-steps-forward-then-three-steps-back—fashion, and that it is the very thing that feels like backsliding to you that will open up the possibility for the next leap forward in your work.

Finally, I ask two things of you as you go through the exercises. First, be ruthlessly honest with yourself, don't let yourself get away with anything. Second, I ask that you approach this work with a great deal of patience and lots of compassion, for your partners and for yourself!

• • • • • • • •

*When I asked Sarah, age 4,
why she was so frustrated
while watching a popular
children's TV show, her reply was:*

*"I hate this show! They always
say they're going to do something
and then they never really do it.
I HATE THAT!"*

The Reality of Doing

There is a great mistake, something is very wrong in the theatre today. The majority of our theatre is a theatre where nothing is really happening, nothing is really happening *right now*. Not only is *right now* all that we have available to us in life, it is absolutely the key to *LIFE* on the stage. Yet most actors are reproducing what has been done before. Attempting to repeat what "clicked" in rehearsal or to recapture what "wowed!" last night's audience.

This raises a wonderful question about one of our jobs as actors. How do we create "the first time" every time we perform the play? Clearly, the audience is paying to see the first time tonight not *last night* tonight. Yet, we have rehearsed the play, made a multitude of choices, we've learned the words and mastered the blocking. So, "We already know." When the surprise knock comes at the door in act two, we know, and, we must not know.

The actor must not know. So how do we "not know," not anticipate, not get ahead of where we are. (and not get ready for that
big moment in the next scene while in the middle of this scene!)

The answer is really very simple (well, simply said. Or as Sandy
said about acting, "It's really very simple—just takes a lot of
years to learn.") The way to make it look like the first time is for
it to be the first time and to achieve this we must be living fully
in the present. For when I am with you *right now* it truly is the
first time and I no longer need to make it "look like." (What a
challenge when so much of our lives are spent in the illusion of
the past and the future, as if they were real. Or as someone I
once heard said, *"It's as if we are driving down the highway of life
looking in the rearview mirror!"*) In fact we must never be "making it look like" on stage. What then do we do?

Sadly, for the most part, what I see in the theatre are actors who
are not *really doing* anything. Acting is doing. It is not talking
about—it is really doing. (By the way, very few directors know
about this.) Sanford Meisner created a meticulous and expansive
process, a step-by-step, organic and healthy approach to the
craft of acting. He told us that: "The seed to the craft of acting
is the reality of doing." *The seed*, there could be no better anal-
ogy, for this seemingly simple statement continually unfolds
with each step of the journey, it is the spine for all of the work.

And yes, I did say a "healthy" approach. Healthy because the
work is grounded in who we are today, not who we once were
or what we once may have experienced. Also, and especially,
because the whole realm of the actor's emotions and the emotional instrument is handled in a way unlike most other techniques. In this approach our emotions come freely, as a side ben-
efit, a gift, when our attention is on something else and that
something else *is what we are doing*. The great news here is that

when our attention is not on being emotional, our emotions suddenly become much more available.

You know, there are too many so-called acting classes which are actually therapy sessions disguised as acting classes. Teachers who instigate or push the student to "get emotional" and leave the student open and raw, without a sense of purpose or closure. I have worked with many students who have been damaged by this kind of work. What I want you to know is that acting is not emoting. Again, ACTING IS NOT EMOTING. Acting is *doing something.* Of course acting does demand of us the ability to access our own rich emotional life and the way in, the organic way, is through meaningful doing.

· · · · · · · · ·

In the 1930s, in New York City, a man named Harold Clurman, out of his unbound passion and his tremendous dissatisfaction with the theatrical experience in this country, brought together some of the finest theatre artists of his time to create a company which would totally and fantastically alter the American theatre. They called themselves The Group Theatre, and in the relatively short time they were together, from 1931 until 1940, they brought a depth of spirit, a fervent life and soul to the stage that was unlike anything American audiences had ever witnessed. They were committed to building a new kind of theatre that was truly collaborative and which spoke to the moral and social issues of their time. Many greats of the theatre came out of the Group's founding company—one of them was Sanford Meisner.

When we think of American acting prior to the Group and look at the examples we have in the silent films, we think of large, cliche gestures and exaggerated posing. And though the Group Theatre members transformed acting in this country some 60 years ago, I believe the work that we are tackling here is still revolutionary. For though the old gestures may be out, the new postures are in. A real moment in the theatre is extremely hard to find and when it does happen it is often the result of an accident on stage—a prop was misplaced, the arm of a chair falls off, or due to the rain and a leaky ceiling, the actors are dripped on. For most actors these are disasters because they are unplanned, not "set" in rehearsals—rather than embraced as a wonderful surprise, simply something new to work-off, to respond to!

I remember a scene in a play I saw a number of years ago. The female lead walked away from the two men she was in conversation with downstage right to go to a table that was upstage left. Though the two men were still talking, my attention went with the woman as she approached the table and on the table, a tray with a bottle of brandy and four glasses. When she arrived and began to reach for the brandy, she had a most wonderful, authentic moment (the only one in this play) of sheer terror as she discovered that the three glasses were already filled! She froze in a state of panic as she tried to think of a way to handle the situation. She finally picked up the bottle and proceeded to tilt it just enough over each glass so that it would look like she was really pouring. Now wouldn't it have been much simpler to notice that the glasses were already filled and then to simply serve them?

Isn't it so much *simpler* and doesn't it make so much more sense when reading a letter on stage to *actually read that letter* rather than to pretend to read a piece of paper with squiggly lines on it. With squiggly lines you must remember to move your eyes in the correct manner to make it look like you *are* actually reading. Why not actually read? Less to think about and much less effort, your eyes will look like they are reading because they are reading and you don't have to work at making the audience believe you. You know what? You can never make an audience believe you, you can only invite them to share your experience.

actually do it

These examples are useful to illustrate, at a very basic level, this thing called the *reality of doing*. When you do something, you don't pretend to do it, you really do it. As I said earlier, this is the underpinning to all of our work, for ultimately when we are supposed to be madly in love in a moment of the play, we must *BE* madly in love in that moment. When we are supposed to be enraged, we must actually be enraged. (Of course, you might ask about stabbing the hero, watching a distant sunset, or getting drunk on stage. I'm sure you've already determined that we don't actually do these things on stage. It is when we have made the meaning of these acts extremely personal and specifically meaningful that we are able to accept them and live them out *as if* they are real. With this acceptance, the impact they have on us, IS REAL!)

And though many directors are concerned with projection, not many are aware that it is only, I'll say that again, *it is only* with the actors actual experience on stage that we reach every seat in the house, reach every person where they live. I know this is true. As Sandy told us, it is never about being bigger, it is always about going deeper.

I want to give you a very simple experience of the reality of doing. Look at the following two numbers than close your eyes and in your minds eye, not on paper, multiply the two numbers. The two numbers are:

7948 X 6988.
Do it now and then read on.

• • • • • • •

Let me ask you a few questions. Did you do it? Did you try to do it or did you quickly give up? Did you get the answer? Was it very difficult and still you gave it your best shot? Listen, the answer doesn't matter, it's never about the results. It's always about the attempt. IT IS ALL IN THE ATTEMPT. And while you tried, who was doing the multiplying? Was it you? Was it you as Gregory Peck in *To Kill a Mockingbird* or you as Joanne Woodward in *Rachel Rachel?* Or were YOU MULTIPLYING? Though you didn't get the answer, were YOU REALLY DOING THAT?

I didn't do it (shame on me)

I bet, if you really tried, something happened to you. You might have noticed yourself laughing, grunting, feeling hopeless, or having some other response to this nearly impossible task. If so, were you pretending to have that response to impress me? Of course not, I'm just a book! You responded however you did because you were really trying to multiply. YOU CAME TO LIFE because you were really doing something! And you didn't have to force or push or even think about having an emotion. Your authentic response was out of your control while your attention was on what you were doing. Remember that!

• • • • • • • •

A WARM UP

I want you, as a group, to do the following little game together. It's a story-telling game and it works like this: Sit in a circle and get real tight together, pick a person who will begin the story, and pick a direction the story will go around the circle. Now the rules are that each person may only say one word and as you go around the circle, you must tell a story. So, do you have your person who will begin and the direction? Good. Now if anyone says more than one word, you must stop and start a new story. Go ahead and give it a try. Do it for a while and when you can't bare it any longer, keep it going. Then, at some point, stop and read on.

• • • • • • • •

I want you to do it again and this time I want you to know that your mission is to become like one person telling a story. That means that you must take out all the pauses between each person. So let the story whip around the circle. This requires that you not try to *take the story* but that you allow the story *to take you*. Also, you may find the story very funny at times. (Did you all end up on the floor laughing?) Great to have a response to what is happening but when it gets in the way of what you are trying to accomplish, not so great. So, this time take out all pauses and become like one person telling a story. Go ahead and do that for about ten minutes.

· · · · · · · · ·

Try it one more time with two additions. First, the story must include two main characters. You will discover them as you tell the story. Second, tighten up your circle, get real close and this time I want you to do it with your eyes closed. Go ahead and do that now and then read on.

· · · · · · · · ·

To achieve your goals in this game, what does it require of you? Well, what happens if you try to prepare with a word when the story is on the other side of the circle or, in other words, try to make the story go where you want it to go? By the time the story gets to you, your word might not fit anymore, isn't that true? So, a big part of this game is about a giving up of control isn't it? Also, not anticipating, because in this game you really cannot prepare. In fact the more you prepare, the less you are able to tell the story! It's only in that moment, when the person right next to you gives you their word, that you will discover what comes out of your mouth.

What then must you be doing? *You must be listening* and you know what? The more you are listening the less you will be preparing, controlling. The success of this game comes from *really listening* and *taking what you get.* The more you can do this, the more you will trust that a word will in fact come out of your mouth and that with that word, you will tell the story.

Having said all that, give it one more try with eyes open and then read on.

· · · · · · · ·

REPETITION
The First Step

Our working definition of acting is, "Acting is living truthfully under imaginary circumstances." *Living Truthfully.* After the years I have spent working in the theatre, I keep coming back to the profound power and beauty of this very simple phrase. It is the core of our work together.

More of our acting comes from our true listening (another way of saying that is *being fully available*) than from anything else. Our fuel on stage is our partners, the other actors, so that we must be open and receptive to them at all times. Even in the midst of the most extreme and heightened moments, it is imperative that we be present to our partners and our environment in every moment (the stage is a dangerous place!). Isn't this great! If I turn myself over to my PARTNER and instead of pushing, give up control, I get everything I need (like a good relationship). Yet most actors make acting very effortful, doing it on their own in spite of their partners on stage, isolated in their own private experience (like bad relationships).

Now, with our first step, "repetition", we are going to bring this whole thing called acting down to its simplest level. In doing so, I am going to take a number of things away from you. Just as in the scales for a pianist, many of the keys cannot be played. The musician is not playing ANYTHING, he's playing THIS

SCALE. It is by the specific structure or boundary of the scale that ultimately he is set free. The scales will disappear and what remains is the musician IN the music. Same thing with repetition. I will give you some specific rules to follow, a structure which, down the road, will disappear and what will be left is you in your acting.

Today, I will also give the first instructions to the "Observer." Very simply, the Observer will be assisting and supporting the Partners who are at work in the exercise. Many times, those who are working will be unable to "see" the things they are doing, or not doing, that are getting in the way of their own progress. The Observer's main job will be to help each partner become aware of what is happening. Change begins with awareness! As your skills grow as you actually do the acting exercises, you will also grow in your effectiveness as the Observer.

Throughout the book, I will be giving the Observer specific things to be watching for as well as ways to interact with the partners who are doing the work. You may be uncomfortable playing the Observer, giving feedback when you don't really "have it all down yet" yourself. That's great. What a great space to be in. What a great place for true learning to occur! Listen, will you make mistakes? Probably. Is it okay to make mistakes? Absolutely! If you simply say what you see and stick to your own simple truth, you'll do just fine. So, be honest and be direct.

Exercise 1. MECHANICAL REPETITION

1. Take two chairs and place them facing toward each other.
2. You and your partner each sit down in a chair so that you are both facing each other. Have a little room between the two of you.
3. Pick one person to start the exercise. We'll call you Partner A.

4. For Partner A: First I want you to turn your head away from your partner (who we will call Partner B).

To the Observer: After you read through to Step 5, when Partner A has turned his or her head away, you will take a moment and then say "Begin" or "Go" to start the exercise. The Observer will continue to do this throughout today's Session.

Partner A, when you hear "Begin" or "Go" from the Observer, turn your head back and say outloud the *very first thing* you ACTUALLY NOTICE over there on your partner. This must be a *physical observation*. (For example, if the first thing I was aware of as I looked at my partner were her eyes, I would say "eyes" or if it was her green sweater I would say "green sweater.") Again it is whatever you ACTUALLY notice and not what you might conjecture. So you would not say, "You had a bad day" or "You don't like me" and so forth.

5. Go ahead and try that a few times, waiting for the Observer to get you started. Then switch and Partner B try that a few times. Then read on. *So strange*

• • • • • • • •

What you just practiced was something called *taking the first thing*. It is an extremely important element in our work. When you look over at your partner, you must say the very first thing that you are aware of. You also must become aware of when you don't do that. What I mean is that you must notice when you see something and you don't say it and then look for something else to observe so that you can say that. This usually happens very quickly, so quickly that you might not be aware of it. So now, I am asking you to bring it into awareness. Are you saying the very first thing that you notice over there?

To the Observer: You must help them here by pointing out to the partner who starts when they did not use the very first thing they were aware of. Stay relaxed in your attention, what I mean is, don't strain to see if it happens, trust that you will notice it if it does. When you do notice this occurring, simply say, "Start again and take the very first thing you are aware of." Do this throughout today's session.

Try Step 5 again with this information. You might start to overly watch yourself for a few moments, that's OK for right now. Go ahead and each of you try Step 5 a few more times and then proceed to Step 6.

· · · · · · · ·

6. The next step:

Now, start again with Partner A making the physical observation. After Partner A begins, I want Partner B to repeat what you hear. So if Partner A says "green sweater," Partner B will say "green sweater." Then Partner A, I want you to repeat what you hear, "green sweater," and now Partner B, you repeat what you hear, "green sweater," and you keep going, *always repeating what you hear.* Simple, right? Yes it is. Simply repeat what you hear, do nothing else. Now put Step 5 and 6 together. Partner A starts and makes the observation which begins the repetition and then you continue repeating, *always repeating what you hear.* Also, ONCE YOU BEGIN, KEEP THE REPETITION GOING AND DO NOT DROP OUT OF THE REPETITION UNTIL THE OBSERVER SAYS TO STOP! NO MATTER WHAT!

To the Observer: You will tell them when to stop. Keep varying the length of each exercise so that those working won't begin to anticipate when it is getting near the end. Sometimes it might be painfully long and other times a number of seconds. And anywhere in-between. As they are working, the partners may begin to have all kinds of responses to the work. Certainly allow the repetition to continue through these and see where it leads.

Go ahead and give it a try, each partner having a chance to start the repetition at least three times. Do it now, then read on.

· · · · · · · ·

Some things to be aware of at this point:

While working, did you notice the word changing at all or did your partner add another word or even a sound to what was being said? Did any mistakes occur to the word you started with as you were repeating? You know what, <u>THERE ARE NO MIS-TAKES</u>. (It's the same on stage—there are no mistakes, you must accept and embrace everything that happens!) The rule is: Take what you get from your partner and repeat exactly what you hear. So if your partner changes "circle on the shirt" to "shirkle on the cert" you must repeat "shirkle on the cert." Do you then work your way back to "circle on the shirt?" No, what is in the past is over and dead, all you have is what is happening right now and you work from that.

To the Observer: if either partner does not repeat exactly what the other person just gave to them, stop the exercise and ask if they were aware of what was just said to them. If not, tell them what they missed and then begin again. Also, alternate who starts the exercise.

Nth less

How will you know if they heard it and didn't repeat it? Because you heard it. You see, from your seat, you are really doing repetition with both partners. (Not out loud, of course.) Make sure they are precise in repeating exactly what was given to them.

Listen, this is new for you too, you may miss some changes. That's OK, do the best you can, right? Your awareness as the Observer will continually grow. Also, this does not mean they should be repeating a cough or a laugh, this gets you more into the area of mimicking, which is talked about in the next pointer.

Important note: When you were repeating, were you *copying* your partner? In other words, were you mimicking how your partner said what he or she said? If so, don't. It's not about copying the quality of how it is said, it is simply about repeating what you hear. How it comes out of your mouth, leave alone. That's a lot simpler, isn't it?

Did you notice anything happening with you as you repeated? Did you laugh or want to laugh or did you both laugh together? Any other responses? If so, what did you do with your experience—did you try to get yourself back together so that you could do the exercise right? The rule here is to have whatever experience you *have* and *repeat*. If you start laughing, great—laugh and repeat. If you're bored, be bored and repeat. By the way, do you have an idea as to where your response came from? If you said the other person you are correct! What was happening with you came from your connection with each other, a connection which occurs as you really listen to each other. (Remember, listening is doing.) Also notice how naturally, simply, and on their own these responses happened. That's GREAT!

To the Observer: Your job here is to keep the repetition going. Whatever response the partners have to repeating with each other is fantastic, AND, do not let them give up the repetition. For example, Partner A may laugh so hard that she has a hard time speak-

ing. Help her to have her response and to repeat, allowing the words to come out however they come out AS SHE LAUGHS. Do you get that? You can yell something like, "DON'T DROP THE REPE- TITION!" And if it takes yelling to be heard, YELL! Make sure you are heard! Also, watch for, if in the midst of a large response like this, this partner drops out of listening to the other person. You can say, "Put your attention back on your partner and repeat!"

When the Observer interacts with those of you who are work- ing, do not come out of the exercise. Simply take the note the Observer just gave you, keeping your attention on your partner, and keep going. Remember, never drop out of the exercise until the Observer says to stop.

Never do anything more than is actually happening. What I mean is, <u>be aware of any desire to *be interesting*</u>. Do not pur- posely do anything with the words. Leave yourself alone and repeat what you hear. Your attention must be over there with your partner.

As soon as you hear what you hear, repeat what you hear. Take out any pausing that might be occurring between hearing what you hear and your repeating it. This is not technical, it is not about "pacing," it is simply, there is nothing to think about so when you hear what you hear, repeat what you hear. This does not mean rushing. You must not be "topping" what your part- ner is saying or in other words, repeating what he is saying before he has actually finished saying it.

Why do you think this is important? If you jump in too soon, you are working from the assumption that you already know what your partner is going to say. You are assuming that what has happened before will happen again. (Like in life when we "already know them" the relationship is dead.) Do you see that? She may have said "curly hair" the last twenty times but isn't it possible, isn't it POSSIBLE that this time she will say something else? (Though your father has always put down and mocked psychotherapy, is it possible that today he will have a session with a therapist? Yes it is. It is possible.) An actor must *never assume anything!* You never know what your partner will say until they have said it. So don't wait and don't rush, simply repeat what you hear when you have heard it.

*To the Observer: The partners who are repeating may not be aware that they are pausing or that they are topping each other. Help them take the pauses out by saying, "As soon as you hear it, repeat it" or "Take out the pauses." If they are topping each other you can say, "Don't rush, really listen!" or "Partner B you're topping her, don't work so hard!"

7. Go ahead now and do some repetition. Work for about twenty minutes with each other and then read on.

• • • • • • • •

.

How is that feeling for you? Let me tell you a few keys to all of this work:

Don't do the repetition, let the repetition do you.

Stay relaxed and don't try so hard to get the exercise right. In fact, *trying to do the exercise right is not doing the exercise right!* It is the TRYING that creates a tension which will shut down your true availability.

There is no need to keep the exercise on track because there is no track.

There is no where to get to so you might as well be there. Do you see that? There is truly nowhere to get to! Isn't that a relief? How much of our lives are we trying to get somewhere else? When I do this or that I will have arrived! How often am I actually right where I am? How often am I right here, right now? You see, acting must always be: right now, right now, right now, right now, right now, right now, right now…each "right now" taking us forward. How magnificent when we can stand fully in RIGHT NOW!

We are making acting very simple. You don't have to be a "great actor" to do this, do you? You don't have to be "interesting." In *cat* fact, if you are in any way trying to make the exercise interesting, you will be unable to really do it. You know, Stanislavsky said: "…you are more interesting than the greatest actor that ever lived!" The audience doesn't need another Robert Duvall, we've already got a GREAT ROBERT DUVALL! What they need is a fully authentic, fully alive YOU! I'd like you to do something I do with my "in person" students. Spend a few minutes with your eyes closed, repeating the following three words to yourself, "I am enough." Go ahead, take the time to do that now. OK. Leave it all alone now. Go play some basketball.

• • • • • • • •

HOMEWORK

Between now and Session Two, meet with a partner two times and at each meeting do at least fifteen minutes of repetition.

Also, I want you to take this thing called, "taking the first thing" into your life. What I mean is: As you are walking down the street, shopping at the mall, eating in a restaurant, waiting in line at the bank—whatever it is—you can be practicing taking the first thing. Practicing as you encounter life. If you begin to bring into awareness your first response to people, trees, foods, the sky, and soon, even for a few minutes a day, you will discover that you have a very personal and specific response to everyone and everything. You will find that everyone and everything has meaning to you.

*Be patient toward all that is unsolved
in your heart.
Try to love the questions themselves.*

*Do not now seek the answers
which cannot be given
because you would not be able
to live them.
And the point is,
to live everything.*

*Live the questions now.
Perhaps you will then
gradually,
without noticing it,
live along some distant day
into the answers.*

—Rainer Maria Rilke

Point of View

WARM UP

Do repetition for about fifteen minutes and then read on. (When I give you a length of time, that is for each pair of partners in the group.)

• • • • • • • •

INTO LANGUAGE

We are now going to take a next step with the repetition. For no better way of saying it, I call this step, "putting into language." It is a simple new element in the work and it will raise a few very important issues. It works like this: As I turn to my partner and see her green sweater, rather than saying "green sweater," I might say, "You have a green sweater" or, "You're wearing a green sweater" or whatever words come out of my mouth as I notice the green sweater. So as compared to "green sweater" this is now more like real talk—it is real talk! How you say it is not important, it's however it comes out of your mouth as you notice the first thing. So I might have said, "green sweater on you there" or, "sweater, green sweater you got on." It's however I discover I am saying it as I say it. *Nice*

Now, with this new element in the repetition, go ahead and do some. Each partner start two times, then come back and read on.

• • • • • • • •

Now there are some things to talk about.

First this example to illustrate:

I came to work with my partner today. I am wearing jeans and a grey shirt. She has on black pants and a red shirt. We sit down to do repetition and she begins. She looks over at me and says, "You're wearing a grey shirt." Repeating what I hear, I say, "You're wearing a grey shirt." She says, "You're wearing a grey shirt." And on we go.

As we move into real talk or *really talking to each other* and in beginning our movement away from mechanical-land, we have to deal with one, *what's happening* and two, our *truthful point of view*. Both of these lead you to the first changes that must occur within the repetition.

WHAT'S HAPPENING

Let's look at the example I just gave. Who's shirt was my partner talking about? She was talking to me about my grey shirt. That is what was happening in the moment. So I must now repeat what I hear and include what is happening right now. She said

"*You're* wearing a grey shirt," so I would now repeat, "*I'm* wearing a grey shirt." I repeated what I heard and I changed the "*You're* wearing..." to "*I'm* wearing..." to keep the truth of what was happening, which was about my shirt. (Explaining it is making it sound more complex than it really is, as you will see when you do some more repetition. Let me make a few more points before you work again.)

TRUTHFUL POINT OF VIEW

As I said earlier, all that we have to work from as actors is our truthful point of view and we never give it up. So when I respond to my partner and I repeat, saying "You're wearing a grey shirt" what does she know to be true? She knows that she is wearing a red shirt. What must she than repeat to keep her truthful point of view? She repeats what she heard and changes the repetition to "I'm wearing a red shirt" or, "I'm not wearing a grey shirt." The repetition is changing because IT MUST CHANGE. It changes as she holds on to what she knows to be true. ALWAYS! (And what if you really believed that her shirt was grey? What would you have to repeat back to her?)

Here are a few examples to demonstrate how this makes very simple sense. If my partner has her hands on her lap and I say, "You have your hands on your lap" and then she moves her hands somewhere else, the repetition must change. She might then say, "I don't have my hands on my lap" or "I had my hands on my lap." Let's say my partner has on glasses and I don't. I start with, "You're wearing glasses" and he repeats back to me, "You're wearing glasses." What would I have to say? Well, something like, "I'm not wearing glasses." Got it?

So you see, the repetition can change now. It changes not because you want it to change or you feel like changing it but because it must change as you work from what is happening and from your truthful point of view. Now do some repetition and work with this new information. Each partner begin five times and then read on.

· · · · · · · ·

Other things to be aware of now:

As we bring the repetition into language you are going to come up against some life conditioning. First, your partner may say something to you and you may find yourself pausing to consider. Know that this is the mind's habitual response out of the *need to be right.* The mind's function is survival or in other words, being right.

At this point in your work it is vital to repeat immediately, as you hear what you hear. In this way, if you allow it to, the repetition will take you to what you know to be true, rather than you figuring it out. *Figuring it out* puts you right in your head. (And being in your head is the death of your acting.) Example: My partner says to me "You look like a bull frog." In my mind, I pause to consider, "A bullfrog? What does she mean by that? Oh God, do I look like a bullfrog? Hey, I don't think I like that she said that...oooh, is there something in my nose, and so on. If I repeat immediately, and keep in the repetition with my partner I will not be able to think about it, and may suddenly discover what I know as I hear myself say, "I DON'T LOOK LIKE NO BULLFROG!"

As opposed to what most people think, what we know, takes no thought. An infant communicates to us very specifically and with no thought. "Yeah, but that's instinct!" you may be saying to me. EXACTLY!!! EXACTLY!!!

*To the Observer: When you work again, watch for these pauses of thought and tell the person when it happens. It is so much a habit

and it happens so quickly that it is often hard to notice. All of you must become aware of when you do this. By stopping the exercise and letting the person know they are pausing to think, they will soon let go of this old habit, simply out of the new awareness. Change begins only with awareness.

Right now, you may encounter resistance to saying the first thing. In other words, you are censoring your first response. My partner might look at me and see "big nose" but not want to say it for fear of hurting my feelings. It's not nice to say "You've got a big nose" and it is urgent that she does! Why do you think? In our acting, we must get beyond the *act* you and I have so carefully mastered in life. This is not a good/bad thing and it's not a criticism. It's survival. Most people speak of me as "a very quiet and intense guy." Is that all I am? Of course not, I am all kinds of things, as are you.

In our work together, the beginning of becoming the full expression of ALL that we are, starts with saying the first thing and dropping the nice routine—and I'm not saying don't be nice. You must give up being nice and I AM NOT SAYING DON'T BE NICE. Do you get that? Acting has no room for niceties, reasonableness or "being appropriate." (When you are really living in the present, you are always appropriate!)

Also you must realize that saying the truth to our partners is a gift, always! They now have something real to respond to, OH BOY! They are real with me and I have a real response to that. As opposed to most of life where very little real communication EVER HAPPENS. Why are so many relationships dead or dying? Why are so many employees having heart attacks? How many times have I spent a week going over in my head what I "SHOULD HAVE SAID!" I love what David Mamet says, that people go to the theatre so that they can see that real communication between human beings is still possible. Oh, one more thing. When we don't tell the truth on stage, the audience knows. No matter what you may think, they know!

In a moment, you will do some more repetition. If you are working in a group, those who are watching should start to notice what is going on with the partners who are doing repetition. (I'm planting a seed here!) As the partners repeat, what responses are they having and how would you describe what you see happening with them? (Is something making them excited, or are they bored stiff? Are they relaxed and calm or filled with anxiety?)

To the Observer: At times, when you are aware of something specific happening with one of the partners, stop the repetition and let the group members who are not working, each say what they saw happening with that person, in that moment. Do not discuss it, simply have each person state what they saw happening from their own point of view. ("You got mad" or, "That made you uncomfortable" or, "You really enjoyed that," and so on.) Then have the partners who are working jump back into repetition. By the way, are all of you right in your observations? It's not about being right, it's about what you got from where you are sitting, what you know from your point of view. (Like the twenty witnesses at a bank robbery who have twenty different stories.)

Go ahead now and each do a good ten minutes of repetition. When you have finished, stop. Go get some great Mexican food.

. . . .

HOMEWORK

Before Session Three, meet with a partner a minimum of two times and at each meeting do at least twenty minutes of the repetition.

Inspiration may be a form of super-consciousness, or perhaps of subconsciousness—I wouldn't know. But I am sure it is the antithesis of self-consciousness.

—Aaron Copland

Session Three

What's Happening

WARM UP

Begin today with twenty minutes of repetition and then read on.

• • • • • • • •

THE THREE MOMENT GAME

I want to work with you now on this thing called "What's happening." To do this, I will give you a game to play, a game which is artificial but is useful in that it will serve as a bridge. A bridge which will take us from where we are now to what is next in the work. Here is how the game works: (Read the following and then I'll have you do it.)

- Partner A: In your mind, you will make up a provocative question that you really want to ask your partner. Provocative in the greater sense of the word. The more provocative the better. Then, you will ask your partner the question.
- Partner B: You will repeat the question, just as you have been doing in the repetition, immediately. IMMEDIATELY! And allowing yourself to have, as best you can, whatever response you have to the question. Do not *try* to have a response, simply *allow* whatever response you have to the question as you repeat it.
- Partner A: You will then stop for a moment and describe as best you can what you saw happening over there. What did his or her *behavior* "say to you." Something happened with your partner as he or she repeated the question and it is your job to say what the behavior was, from *your point of view.* Grapple with this outloud and when you have narrowed it down and made it specific, you will state it to your partner directly. That's the end of the game, three moments. One, the provocative question. Two, the response as you repeat the question. Three, stating to your partner what his or her behavior said to you.

Three moments, you see? Here's an example:

Partner A: Does anyone really love you?
Partner B: Does anyone really love me?(As she repeated the question, her eyes looked away, she smiled and giggled.)
Partner A: (Working outloud...) Well there was a gleam in your eyes, but you didn't want me to see it. Your face got red, it's still red. I think the question really embarrassed you, yeah, that was the strongest thing I got. (He ends with a simple, direct statement to her...) That embarrassed you.

psycho analys̃?

End of game. Now the other person asks the question.
Go ahead now and play the Three Moment Game with each

other; each partner ask five questions. Take your time and have fun. Then let's talk about it. Now play, then read on.

· · · · · · · ·

Here are some important things to notice and to be aware of as you do this game. See if any relate to what just happened as you played:

Sometimes you may find yourself, in the third moment, stating back to your partner what you think the answer to the question was.

Partner A: Do you like cleaning toilets?
Partner B: Do I like cleaning *toilets?*
Partner A: You really don't like cleaning toilets!!!

We are not interested here in the answer to the question. What we are interested in is what the behavior said to you. So in this example your statement to your partner might have been, "That made you ill!" or, "You wanna puke!" or whatever it was to you. If you find yourself stating back what you think the answer to the question was, stop and try to figure out what happened with your partner—*what was in their behavior that gave you the answer.*

Do you find yourself using words like "seem" or "look like" as you tell your partner what their behavior said to you. "*You seem* pissed" or "You *look like* you want to scream." You must take "seem" and "look like" and any other modifiers out of your acting vocabulary. Do you have a hunch why this is important?

You know it's a risk to say what we believe to be true. Horrific consequences are possible! The other person may not like us! Or, she may disagree. Or tell us we are just plain wrong. In life "seem" and "look like" and all the others are buffers, a way out. In our acting we want to take away from ourselves any way out, any safety net and we want to say exactly what we mean. So start catching yourself as you do this and stop, then say it over, tell your partner what you got from their behavior without the buffer word.

*To the Observer: If the partners working use the words "you look like," or "you seem" and so on, stop them and tell them so that they can begin to take those words out of their acting vocabulary.

You may be finding, at times, that when your partner repeats your question, you think there is nothing to describe because very little is happening. Listen, THERE IS NEVER NOTH-ING, THERE IS ALWAYS SOMETHING! (It's like your best friend calling you up late on Saturday night and saying, "Hey, I just went on that blind date you set me up on and boy did that girl have no personality!" That really isn't true is it? Isn't there really no such thing as "no personality?" There is always some kind of personality, you see?) All you can do is <u>take what you get</u> and work from that. So if your partner just looks blank to you, you might say, "You're blank" or, "That doesn't do much for you" or whatever words you find.

Did you find this difficult? Are you finding it hard to "read" your partner? It is difficult! We are stretching new muscles here! What I want you to know right now is that what you get from your partner is not simply what you see with your eyes. Sometimes you may get something and not really know how you got it, yet you have a hunch about it. TRUST THAT HUNCH. We'll talk more about this later, now I want you to do some work.

I want you to play the Three Moment Game for twenty min-utes. Then read on.

· · · · · · · · ·

Back to repetition: I now want you to take something away from your repetition. You no longer need to look away from each other to start the repetition. Now, you will sit down facing each other and begin. Who begins? You'll find out as you sit down. Whoever begins, begins. There is nothing to wait for! Whatever is the first thing you get as you sit with each other, is the thing you start with. So the looking away business, to get the first thing, served its purpose and is no longer needed. What I'm saying is, we are through with it so don't do it anymore. (That's very much how this work goes. We are always moving forward, never going back.)

To the Observer: Once the repetition has begun, you will call out the partners' names to have them work from a new observation. Now, the repetition will not stop but will be continuous. So, let's say the repetition is under way and you say, "Nancy Go!" Nancy will immediately say whatever she's aware of over on her partner, in that moment, and the repetition continues—the partners working from this new observation. Then, at some point you say, "Bill Go!" Bill will now immediately say what he observes in that moment and onward they go. And so on... You will continue to do this throughout the exercise. Have fun and be tricky (call the same persons name three times in a row, and so forth) so that the partners cannot anticipate the changes.

Now do ten minutes of repetition for each set of partners.

• • • • • • •

HOMEWORK

Between now and Session Four, meet at least twice with a partner and at each meeting do twenty minutes of the Three Moment Game. Then do ten minutes of repetition.

CLARIFICATION

You may have a question here about how, when you are working on your own, to start from new observations while the repetition is going. Well, as you have just learned, you both sit and one of you will begin. Then, as you are repeating, at some point, the other partner jumps in with their observation and then you both repeat that. Then, at some point, the other partner jumps in with a new observation and so on.

Are you wondering how long you should keep repeating before someone throws in a new observation? Please, don't worry so much about doing this right, remember? Explore! Whenever one of you has a strong impulse to change the repetition because of something you just observed, SAY IT! See where that takes the two of you.

See you at Session Four!

Living is a form of not being sure, not knowing what, next or how. The moment you know how, you begin to die a little. The artist never entirely knows. We guess. We may be wrong, but we take leap after leap in the dark.

—Agnes De Mille

Working-Off

WARM UP

Do ten minutes of the Three Moment Game and then read on.

• • • • • • • •

THREE MOMENT GAME: PART II

You know, what we are doing with the Three Moment Game is crucial. We are isolating this thing called behavior. We are zooming in on behavior and strengthening our ability to really see it. (And I don't mean just with the eyes.) As actors, we really must get on <u>intimate terms</u> with the domain of behavior...

Now, I want you to do the Three Moment Game in the following way. Everything stays the same except for the third moment. Now the third moment must happen immediately. So take out the thinking about what you get from your partner's behavior as they repeat the question and tell them what you got immediately! Then, let that third moment lead you into repetition. Here is an example:

Partner A: Do you stuff your face when nobody is looking?
Partner B: Do I stuff my face when nobody is looking?
Partner A: *(immediately!)* Ooh, that struck a nerve!
Partner B: Ooh, that struck a nerve?
Partner A: Ooh, that struck a nerve!
Partner B: Ooh, that struck a nerve.

And so on, and so on...   *hmm okay*

As you let the third moment lead you into repetition, continue repeating for seven or eight moments only. Do not go on at length as you have done before. OK, you can go ahead now and do the Three Moment Game in this manner for twenty minutes. Work now and then read on.

• • • • • • • •

How does that feel? In the third moment, did you find that sometimes you knew that you got "something?" from your partner but you could not immediately find the words to describe it? That's OK. If you don't have the words you must still respond to what you got from your partner, so, respond in some way. You don't have to say it good and it doesn't have to make sense! So if your partner screams in delight your immediate response might be "WOWEE WOW WOW WOW!" You see, it is better to respond immediately, than to stop to "Get it right" or "Say it well", ALWAYS!   *WOWEE WOW WOW WOW*

I want you to read on into the next section now, as we bring the next element of the repetition into play.

• • • • • • •

REPETITION: WORKING-OFF

I want you each to try something right now.

Do the Three Moment Game as you have just done it, the third moment leading you into repetition. Now as you are repeating, when you are aware of *something happening over there*, something that you get from your partner, you can say it. I am telling you that now, as you are aware of things happening with your partner, you must respond to that—which means that the repetition will now have changes in it. Give that a try and once your into the repetition, don't stop for a while. Simply allow the repetition to change when you are aware of something going on with your partner. Do it now one time and then read on.

•   •   •   •   •   •   •   •

Going back to the example I used before, here is an example of what we are working toward at this point:

Partner A: Do you stuff your face when nobody is looking?
Partner B: Do I stuff my face when nobody is looking?
Partner A: *(immediately!)* Ooh, that struck a nerve!
Partner B: Ooh, that struck a nerve?
Partner A: Ooh, that struck a nerve!
Partner B: Ooh, that struck a nerve.
Partner A: Yeah, that struck a nerve!
Partner B: Oh you think you got me.
Partner A: Oh I think I got you!
Partner B: Yeah, you think you got me.
Partner A: Yeah, I think I got you!
Partner B: You're proud of that.
Partner A: I am proud of that!
Partner B: You are proud of that?
Partner A: I am proud of that!!

Partner B: You are proud of that??
Partner A: You're angry.
Partner B: I'm angry.
Partner A: You're angry.
Partner B: I am angry!
Partner A: You admitted it.
Partner B: I admitted it.
Partner A: You admitted it.
Partner B: So I admitted it!
Partner A: You are really defensive.
Partner B: I am really defensive.
Partner A: Yeah, you're defensive.
Partner B: I'm not defensive.
Partner A: You are defensive.
Partner B: I'm not defensive.
Partner A: You are defensive.
Partner B: Sticking to your guns, huh.
Partner A: Sticking to my guns, huh?
Partner B: Sticking to your guns!
Partner A: Sticking to my guns?
Partner B: You don't understand.
Partner A: I don't understand.
Partner B: You don't understand.
Partner A: I don't understand!
Partner B: You really mean that.
Partner A: I do mean it.
Partner B: You do mean it.
Partner A: I do mean it.
Partner B: You do mean it.
Partner A: You're really taking me in.
Partner B: I'm really taking you in.

And so on...

What we are getting into now is *working-off*, becoming available to what is happening with our partner and being in response to that. I want you each to do twenty minute of repetition now, working-off your partner.

*To the Observer and All Group Members: You all must now be active participants, working in your seats. You must, at all times, be "working-off" the two partners who are doing repetition, sitting on the edge of your seats improving your own ability to work-off behavior. You must not be sitting back passively waiting to be entertained! The question is, what are you getting from where you are?

Work now, twenty minutes for each set of partners and then let's talk.

• • • • • • • •

As you did the repetition, did you find periods of working with each other where the repetition went on for a long time and it didn't change? Do not worry about that at this point. It is better for that to be happening right now then to be *looking for the next thing* or *trying* to make the repetition change. You see, this is all very new to you right now, so you will be missing moments, not getting all that is coming your way. Your work, as you keep doing the repetition, is to become more fully available to each moment as it happens.

How do you do that? Let me tell you something, you cannot *MAKE* yourself more available, you can only invite it and encourage it to occur. The repetition is your vehicle. It will take you there if you do the things I have told you. Again, work consistently and "Don't do the repetition, let the repetition do you", which, right now means: Repeat immediately and keep your attention on your partner. In this way you cannot get ahead of yourself and you will *discover* when the repetition must change rather than trying (efforting) to find the things to change it to. Did you find that, at times, you were aware of yourself having thoughts during the repetition? A lot of times these thoughts are the very thing you could have said to your partner but didn't, so you end up thinking about it. For example: You feel that your partner is "taking control" and you hear yourself repeating automatically (like a robot) for a good many moments while in your head you are thinking, "God, he's controlling this thing!" There are two things to do:

First, you must begin to allow that voice in your head to be expressed to your partner, "God, you're controlling this thing!" You see, that's the repetition!

Or second, if the moment has passed, you must bring your attention back to your partner and what is happening *right now.*

So if you're thinking "What a great smile" and by the time you realize you've been thinking this for a while she's looking very serious, you work-off *right now* "You are very serious."

ADHD

Listen, the mind is extremely seductive, so you must bring it to awareness when you are getting lost in thought and out of sheer will, bring yourself back to your partner. It's hard work now, but ultimately, it will all be like tying your shoes—you won't have to think about it!

Each person do another ten minutes of repetition and then call it a day.

• • • • • • • •

HOMEWORK

Between now and Session Five, meet at least twice with a partner and at each meeting do one-half hour of repetition as we have just been doing, *working-off your partner.*

"*The* right art," cried the master, "is purposeless, aimless! The more obstinately you try to learn how to shoot the arrow for the sake of hitting the goal, the less you will succeed in the one and the further the other will recede. What stands in your way is that you have a much too willful will. You think that what you do not do yourself does not happen."

"...How can the shot be loosed if I do not do it?" I asked the master.

"It shoots," he replied.

—From, *Zen In The Art Of Archery*
by Eugen Herrigel

Working-Off, Continued

WARM UP

Do a good ten minutes of repetition for each person and then read on.

• • • • • • • •

REALLY TALK / REALLY LISTEN

In the repetition exercise, in all of this work, we must continually be leaving the exercise behind, giving up the "exerciseness" of it. I know this sounds strange when you are working so hard to "get" the exercise. You must keep moving yourself from repetition as some kind of trick you can do, toward your fully *being with* another human being. (Believe me, this work is not about becoming a great repeater!) Our aim, right now, is in you becoming fully available to your partner, authentically responsive in each moment. This starts right now with—really talk, really listen, really talk, really listen... really talk to each other, really listen to each other.

Here's something I want you to hear again—don't try so hard. You do not need to find the things to work-off, your partner will give them to you, always. You simply have to BE THERE. Also, you work-off everything. It can be behavior ("You are very sad") it can be a physical observation ("funky red tie!") it is whatever you get in the moment. Do not pass over anything, it's all grist for the mill. If you think something is not worth working-off, *you're in your head.*

The rule here is:

Don't do anything unless something makes you do it. And right now the *something* is over there. I'll say that again,

Don't do anything unless something makes you do it and *right now* the something is *over there.*

As you continue, stay relaxed. (I mean, what's the worst that could happen? The Repetition Patrol is not going to come and get you!) Don't push and *take what you get.*

Each partner will do another ten minutes of repetition right now and that's all for today.

• • • • • • • •

HOMEWORK

Between now and Session Six, meet at least twice and at each meeting do a half hour of repetition.

KNOWING WHAT IS HAPPENING

When you cannot see what is happening in a group, do not stare harder. Relax and look gently with your inner eye.

When you do not understand what a person is saying, do not grasp for every word. Give up your efforts. Become silent inside and listen with your deepest self.

When you are puzzled by what you see or hear, do not strive to figure things out. Stand back for a moment and become calm. When a person is calm, complex events appear simple.

To know what is happening, push less, open out and be aware. See without staring. Listen quietly rather than listening hard. Use intuition and reflection rather than trying to figure things out.

The more you can let go of trying, and the more open and receptive you become, the more easily you will know what is happening.

Also, stay in the present. The present is more available than either memories of the past or fantasies of the future.

So attend to what is happening now.

—From *The Tao Of Leadership,*
Leadership Strategies For A New Age
by John Heider

PINCH AND OUCH

WARM UP

Everyone do a good ten minutes of repetition, then read on.

• • • • • • • •

MOVING FORWARD

We must move forward in the repetition. The "What's happening" will now include not only what's happening over there with my partner, but also, what does what's happening over there, *do to me?* So the what's happening is now *over there* and over here. This is what Sandy called the "Pinch and Ouch". *ok Sandy!*

As we are working with our partner, things add up. You know, saying the same thing seven times, if you are *really talking with each other*, will get monotonous or tedious or infuriating or

SOMETHING! (Just imagine your mother telling you five times, "Why don't you get a real job!") In the exercise, you must respond to this when it happens. "This is boring," "You keep on saying that," "You're on automatic" and so forth.

Your partner says to you, "You look jerky" five times. If you are really listening, this must have an impact on you. I don't know what it would be for you, but if you didn't like it, you'd have every right to say to your partner "Don't say that again!" So there's a Pinch: "You look jerky!" And an Ouch: "Don't say that again!" You see, "Don't say that again!" wasn't something you wanted to say or thought you should say, it was something you had to say because of what you got from your partner and what that did to you. There is a voice in you that wants to speak, allow it! Say it!

I must be careful here. I want to be sure that you do not limit this concept of "Pinch and Ouch" to any one connotation. Look at these examples:

The pinch might be a beautiful smile on your partner's glowing face and the ouch might be your response, "WOW, what a great smile!"

The pinch might be an encouraging, "You are so bright," from your partner and the ouch is your response, "You make me feel great!"

The pinch from your partner, "You really hurt my feelings" and the ouch is your response, "I'm so sorry."

Cause → effect

Hey, doesn't this all sound more like real people—real people really talking with each other? Yes it does and you will! You will surprise yourself in many wonderful ways as you more closely work-off of each other, the more you live moment-to-moment, and as you continue to grow into the full expression of who you truly are. *WHO YOU TRULY ARE!* Not who others want you to be and not who you think you should be but who you *must be* because of what your partner just did and what that did to you. Then you will find that you are moving away from "repetition land" and towards "human being land!"

Careful now! Careful! Do not interpret this to mean that the repetition will now become, in any way, "conversational" or "casual." Remember, you are playing the scales and the scales have their rules. Remember: "Don't do anything unless something makes you do it." I have simply said that now, the "something" is not only *over there* it is also *over here.* I have simply added to the repetition that, when you are aware of it, you must work not only from what you get from your partner but also from what that does to you!

Did you hear that? WHEN YOU ARE AWARE OF IT. The temptation will be to TRY TO DO what I have just talked about. You mustn't! You must not try to do it. It is all about allowing it to occur. ALLOWING...

To the Observer: In a moment we will work. As the partners repeat, watch for responses in each person that are not being expressed. Stop them at these times and ask the person, "What did that just do to you?" The partner can then grapple with, out loud, what was happening for him or her. Then they can begin the repetition with a fresh start.

Or you might tell them what you just got from their behavior. For instance you might stop the exercise and say: "Ted, you really didn't like when June said that you were being too loud." Allow Ted to respond to you: "Yeah, you're right, it made me feel small and I kept thinking that I'd like to just shut her up." Then you can coach Ted in this way: "Well, say that to her right now and continue, let's go!" which will put them back into the repetition. Even though you have stopped for a moment, most of the time, that response is still living and the partners can easily get right back into the exercise.

With this new information, I want you all to do fifteen minutes of repetition. Then read on…

• • • • • • • •

We have now developed a wonderful basis for a specific kind of improvisation, haven't we! As opposed to most acting class improvisations where everyone is in their head thinking of the next clever thing to say, in this improvisation you not only must not be thinking, you are continually given what to say *by your partner,* so there is nothing to think about. GREAT!

• • • • • • •

HOMEWORK

Get together as often as possible and do repetition. Please don't think about doing it. Do it!

Almost anybody can learn to think or believe or know, but not a single human being can be taught to be.

Why?

Because whenever you think or you believe or you know, you are a lot of other people: but the moment you are being, you're nobody but yourself.

To be nobody but yourself—in a world which is doing its best night and day to make you everybody else—means to fight the hardest battle which any human being can fight, and never stop fighting.

Does this sound dismal? It isn't. It's the most wonderful life on earth.

—e.e. cummings

COMING TO THE DOOR

As we established earlier, acting is living truthfully under imaginary circumstances. So far we have addressed which part of this statement? Well so far, we have been working on living truthfully. Right?

Now, I want to add a new element to the exercise. For this you will need a room with a door. If you are working at home, you might use the front door or the door to the living room. If you are working in a studio, you need some basic furniture including a couch, a table and some chairs. Having some other things such as a dresser and small bed are also useful.

The exercise will work this way:

- Partner A, you are in your room.
- Partner B, you go outside the door, close the door behind you, wait a few moments and then knock.

• Partner A, you respond to the knock.

Everything else we have been doing remains the same, in other words, you do repetition as you have been learning to do it. The difference is that now instead of being in chairs facing each other, (and I bet you thought we'd never get out of those chairs!) *6*) one person is in their room and the other person is at the door and he or she knocks. So now choose who will be in their room and who will be at the door.

Before you begin, a few questions. First of all, what have we just added to the exercise? Answer this question in your notebook and then read on. *interesting*

• • • • • • • •

Remember, acting is living truthfully under imaginary circumstances and up until this point we have been working on the "living truthfully." Now we are adding the "imaginary circumstances" to the exercise.

So, to the person in the room—what are you doing in your room? You are not "doing" anything, you are simply in your room. Are you waiting for your partner to knock? No, you are simply in your room. Do you know that your partner or anyone else is coming to see you? No, you are simply in your room. When you hear a knock, is it your partner knocking? You don't know who is there. All you know is that you are in your room and if you hear a knock, you respond to that knock. When you open the door, what is your relationship to the person at the door? Your relationship is whatever it actually is, no more, no less. *with my character sheet*

To the person at the door—when you knock, who do you expect to answer the door? You do not expect anyone to answer because you don't know if anyone is home. You do know who's door you've come to and that's all you know. So, what are you coming to do? You're not coming to do anything, you simply come to the door and knock.

Isn't that simple? I'll ask you one other question. Isn't it true that, in fact, *you do know* that your partner is outside the room and that he or she is coming to the door at some point? To the person outside, isn't it true that *you do know* that the person in the room is actually in there? Must you then believe these imaginary circumstances? Is acting believing? No, it is accepting the imaginary circumstances and living them out as if they are true. You do know and you MUST NOT KNOW. You see, you must ACCEPT that you don't know, an actor MUST NEVER KNOW. We are now going to strengthen this thing called "ACTOR'S FAITH" or the ability to fully accept the imaginary circumstances.

So, what do you do? Well, when the door opens, you do repetition just as you have been doing it, the only difference is that you are not in your seats—you are at the door. The door opens and you "take the first thing" and off you go. Oh, I must tell you that in this exercise, you accept as a given that the door is always locked. Understand? The door is always locked. (Makes it impossible to sit on your couch and yell, "Come on in!" doesn't it!)

Go ahead now and do some work. Try this a few times and then read on.

• • • • • • • •

Some thing to be aware of at this point: When you opened the door, was your first response "Hi", or "Come on in", or "Have a seat", or any other similar comments? You must give up playing the good host or hostess. (Sandy used to yell to us, "'Hi' is for taxi drivers!") What you must do is work off your partner. So when the door opens, one of you will begin the repetition immediately with whatever you get from your partner, just as you have been learning to do. I want you to know that theatre is not an imitation of life, it demands a greater truth! This is where you will begin to learn what that statement is all about.

As you opened the door, did the person outside the door ever barge right in and then once he or she was in, did you both find yourselves not knowing what to do so you quickly headed for the chairs or the couch to sit? Listen, don't do anything unless something makes you do it, remember? Stay with your partner, it's all over there. So, for the person who knocked—did you get from your partner that you should come in? And, if you aren't welcomed in, what is the impact of being kept outside the door and what is your response to that? If you are both at the door or inside the door, where ever you are, stay with what's happening until something really makes you do something else.

You know, it is uncomfortable to stand at the door and simply *be* with each other. Almost everything in us wants to do something, to get comfortable— "Quick, I gotta go find a good seat!" You know, we got used to those two chairs and now they're gone. This work is about continually "letting go of" and being *right here, right now.* In other words, this work IS UNCOMFORT-ABLE. It's about living in the unknown. There you are at the door with this person, not knowing what is going to happen or where simply being with each other is going to take you —TER-RIFYING!—you give up control—OH MY GOD!—and there is nothing to do. So what do you do when you are there at the door and you are feeling so uncomfortable you could scream? You scream, "THIS IS UNCOMFORTABLE!" What about the repetition? That IS the repetition! You just gave your partner something real to work-off, GREAT! Now see where that takes the two of you.

OK, I want you to do two exercises. Each of you take a turn being in the room and coming to the door. Allow the exercise to go on for some time and see where working-off each other takes you. Then, stop working today.

· · · · · · · ·

HOMEWORK

Between now and Session Eight, meet two times and at each meeting do two exercises as you have just learned to do. For Session Eight have one person in your group bring with them a wooden broom handle without the broom at the end. The best is if you have an old one or can buy a cheap one and cut it in half. Whichever it is, be certain that you have one.

The three fundamental principles are to accept your feelings, know your purpose, and do what needs doing. The doing is what is important, not the result. Behavior is what counts, not emotion. Not even the results of behavior. What I do is the only thing in life that I can control.

—From *Playing Ball on Running Water*
by David K. Reynolds, Ph.D.

Doing Fully

Before reading on, have each person do two exercises, one time in the room and one time coming to the door. Then continue on into the activity.

• • • • • • • •

THE ACTIVITY

Acting is Doing. It is not talking about, it is doing something and when we are not really doing on stage we have stopped acting. Every character in every play is after something, they are trying to accomplish something and in well-written plays, every character is fighting for their life to get it, to make it happen. (Please read the plays of Clifford Odets!) The part of this process called "activities" continues the training in *really doing* something. I say continues because part of what we have strengthened in repetition is the ability to really listen and listening is a doing.

(Remember this at the next play you see. Are they really listening or are they making it *look like* they are listening. Just as most salespeople are taught, many actors are trained in the "indication" of listening, "Now I make good eye contact, now I really focus on you, now I fully concentrate, and so forth.)

Acting is not about the words, the actor is given the words by the playwright. The actor's job is to provide truthful behavior which bring the words on the page to life. Breathing life into the playwright's words is nothing less than the act of creation itself! And though we are working on the best first steps I know toward fulfilling this acting demand, ultimately the achievement of it is no less mysterious than the journey of giving birth to a child.

Since becoming a father, I have realized how similar the two really are. We know all of the facts; one out of millions, the sperm meets the egg and the mother begins experiencing vast swings of emotional and physical responses, (from depths of pain and fear to the heights of excitement and joy) to the new life inside her. Then, at a moment totally out of the mother's control, working from the child's own innate wisdom, he or she enters the new world. So, we know the facts, the doctors can detail every aspect of this event with formulas and theories and concepts. But not one doctor, not one specialist anywhere, can speak a word to us about the great mystery we call LIFE.

In this regard I think of my other great acting teacher, Suzanne Shepherd. When we had not quite brought a specific and personal life to the text, Suzanne would yell at us: "Words, words, musical fruit!" I heard Marianne Williamson, in a lecture she gave on spiritual laws, say something that directly links to this discussion, "Nothing occurs on the visible plane that did not first occur invisibly."

Peter Brook speaks about this aspect of acting in his book *The Empty Space* in a chapter called "The Deadly Theatre". He says, " A word does not start as a word—it is an end product which begins as an impulse, stimulated by attitude and behavior which dictate the need for expression. This process occurs inside the dramatist; it is repeated inside the actor. Both may only be conscious of the words, but both for the author and then for the actor, the word is a small visible portion of a gigantic unseen formation. Some writers attempt to nail down their meaning and intentions in stage directions and explanations, yet we cannot help being struck by the fact that the best dramatists explain themselves the least. They recognize that further indications will most probably be useless. They recognize that the only way to find the true path to the speaking of a word is through a process that parallels the original creative one. This can neither be bypassed nor simplified." The word is a small visible portion of a gigantic unseen formation. I love that!

The beginning of this really is "point of view." In more advanced elements of acting such as Character Work, we must grapple with the very specific point of view of the character and through what specifically limited vision does she or he look at the world. Now, as you begin your study of the craft, it is essential that you become intimately in touch with your own point of view. As opposed to many peoples' concept of acting as a putting on of masks to become a character, in fact, acting is a taking off of masks to reveal the character and the character is always you.

• • • • • • • •

THE ACTIVITY
The First Step

For the first exercise with the activity, I want you to use the broom handle or long stick of some sort that you brought to today's session.

- Now, one partner stand in the center of the room.
- The other partner, you sit in a chair facing your partner, giving your partner plenty of space to work.
- The standing partner, you take the broom handle and I want you to balance it on the very tip of your left thumb. Not on the nail or the flat side, on the tip, so that your thumb is pointed to the ceiling. Put all of your concentration, everything you've got into balancing the stick. Do it to *master* balancing the stick, like your life depends on it.
- Now, when that partner gets involved in the balancing, I want you, the seated partner, to wait a few moments and then begin repetition.
- Once repetition begins do not stop, do repetition just as you know how to do it. WHAT
- To the partner balancing, where should your attention be? Put all of your attention on BALANCING THE STICK! AND REPEAT! Do not drop the repetition. And, balance the stick as if your life depends on it, do it TO MASTER BALANCING THE STICK!

*To the Observer: Your job at this point is to help the person with the activity to keep their attention, 100%, on what they are doing, as they continue to do the repetition. So, if you notice him or her take any of their attention off of balancing the stick to "work-off" the partner, you must say something like: "Master balancing the stick and repeat, KEEP BALANCING AND REPEAT!" Or if they stop repeating so that they might balance better, you can say: "DON'T DROP THE REPETITION!"

After doing repetition for a while, switch and let the other partner balance the stick. Follow the same directions except this time, balance on the tip of your pinky finger. When the next person does the activity, you make up a specific way that you will balance the stick. Go ahead now and give it a try. Then read on.

. . . .

OK, let me ask a question. As you worked, did you sense that most or all of the changes in the repetition came from the seated partner and that the partner who was balancing, was mostly, merely repeating back what was said? This is usually what happens in the first few exercises with the activity.

So, in a moment, I want you all to do this activity again and what I want the partner who is balancing to know is that, when you are aware of something happening, you can work-off your partner, as you know how to do. This does not mean that you may take your attention off or give up your mission which is to master balancing the stick. It means that as you put 100% of your attention on balancing the stick, when you are aware of it, you will allow yourself to be in response to what you get from your partner. (Remember, working-off does not mean "looking at.")

So, if as you balance the stick your partner laughs and says, "You're a klutz!" Your response might be, "You're laughing at me" or "You're putting me down." If you hear your partner yawn, your response might be, "This is boring you" or "You are tired." Of course, as always, it is not about the words, it is about being in response to what's happening. And as you balance, you must now begin to respond to what is happening without giving up what you are doing.

Go ahead now. Each partner take a turn doing the activity with this additional information.

. . . .

How did that go? I bet that, this time, you were more available to your partner without giving up the activity. We must, at all times, be fully doing what we are doing on stage. Sandy told us that: "The quality of your acting depends on how fully you are doing what you are doing."

This means a total commitment to what we are doing right now and the moment we are doing something else, we are giving 100% of ourselves to the doing of that. The exercise at this point highlights a basic truth which is that it is impossible to do two things *fully* at the same time. Of course this is somewhat new for most of us who in life are usually doing three things at one time ending up *somewhat* doing three things and *fully* doing none. So, you may ask, how then do I do my activity fully and also work-off my partner fully? GREAT QUESTION! Hold on to that one and keep working!

Again: "The quality of your acting depends on how fully you are doing what you are doing."

For your next meeting you must each bring an <u>activity</u> with you. So, what are the elements which make up an activity at this point? The activity must be physically difficult, extremely difficult for you to do, the more difficult the better. For whom? FOR YOU! It doesn't matter that it's very easy for someone else to accomplish. What matters is that it is extremely difficult for *you* to do.

Also, you must know when you have accomplished what you have set out to do, when the activity is complete. This must be specific. For instance, if your activity is to take a deck of playing cards and build a house of cards, you might set it up knowing that you must use, one at a time, every card in the deck, creating a house that is four levels high. "Any house of cards" is general. A four-story house, using every card in the deck, one at a time—that's getting specific. You know what you are working to accomplish and when you've done it! If you are bouncing a ball on a paddle, how do you know when you have mastered it? Well, maybe you set it up so that you must bounce the ball on the paddle 50 times in a row without letting the ball drop to the floor. You see, when you set it up specifically, who will know when you have accomplished what you have set out to do? YOU WILL! This is vital, *you will know,* and you will know what you are doing specifically! So, it is not any number of bounces on the paddle, it is 50 bounces. You are not doing anything, you are doing THIS, SPECIFICALLY! As Stanislavsky said, "*Anything,* is the enemy of art."

Here's a little quiz. Write down in your notebook why the following example is not a good activity. Ready? Here's the activity: to write the great American novel. Go ahead now, answer this question and then come back and read on.

· · · · · · · ·

Writing the great American novel would certainly be very difficult, but is it physically difficult? No, this activity mostly requires a lot of head work, doesn't it. Secondly, how would *you* really know when you have actually written the great American novel? (Even if it gets published, who's to judge, some might say it is, and to others, it's not. And even if they all say that it is, you still might not believe them!)

I used this example because it shows clearly what you must stay away from in setting up your activity. You must make sure that the activity is truly, *physically difficult.* This does not mean strenuous, although it can be, it means *not in your head.* For example, drawing a lifelike portrait with pen and ink of how you remember your sister when she was ten might be very difficult, but *how you remember her* is in your head. Now, if you do the drawing having an old photograph of your sister at ten years old, right there with you on the table to work from—well now you're on to something! You see, now it's not in your head, it's there in front of you. You can see it and you will know when it's lifelike and complete. The completion of your activity must not be vague or fuzzy, it must be clear and concrete.

Two last things: First, for now, I do not want you to use the element of time in the set up of your activity. What I mean is that the activity must be intrinsically difficult for you. Of course, it would make it harder to bounce the ball on the paddle 50 times if you added that you must do it *in under two minutes*. But for now, I do not want you to use a time limit to help make the activity more difficult. Got that?

Secondly, the activity must be extremely difficult to do, the closer to being impossible the better, but not actually impossible. Do you have an idea why this is vital? You see, if you know that the activity is truly impossible to do, what will you really have to work toward? But if there is even the *remotest possibility* that you can accomplish this incredibly difficult task, well, now you're in the activity arena we're talking about!

• • • • • • • •

HOMEWORK

Now get to work on setting up your first activity. Also, between now and your next Session practice repetition at a minimum of two meetings. You can do it coming to the door as well as just sitting in chairs. (Do not do it with an activity yet.) Then, bring your activity with you to your Session Nine and we will continue moving forward in the work.

Do you think I know what art is?
Do you think I'd think anybody knew,
even if they said they did?
Do you think I'd care what anybody thought?
Now if you ask me what we're trying to do
that's a different thing.

—Georgia O'Keeffe

The Activity, Continued

OK, everyone have their activity? We will now go to the next step in building the exercise. Here's how it goes:

- Partner A is in their room and they are doing the activity.
- Partner B goes out. (Partner B, when you go out, take some time out there so that your partner has time to get involved with their activity.
- Then I want Partner B, to come to the door and knock three times, each time in a different way.
- Partner A, you are doing the activity and as you hear the knocks, I want you to describe the knocks out loud to yourself, what the knock "says" to you.
- Partner B, on the third knock, as you knock, open the door and come in. (For the time being, as we use three knocks in the exercise, the door is "not locked". Got that?)
- Immediately, either one of you will begin repetition.

Session Nine

For example:

My partners first knock is a loud and rapid four thuds on my door. I might say to myself (out loud), *"That was an angry knock."* Her second knocks are very soft taps. I might say, *"How gentle."* Her third knock is slow and careful and as she opens the door slowly I say to her, *"You're hesitant,"* which leads us right into repetition. (Of course, depending on the moment, she might begin the repetition as she enters, working-off what she gets from me.)

See what we're doing here? You are working-off of the knock. This isn't mysterious, what it is about is that everything has meaning to you and you must work off of it, be available to it. You see, when you have the activity, the exercise starts the moment you enter your room to accomplish this incredibly difficult task. You are not waiting to do some great repetition with your partner! You don't even know that anyone is coming over! Remember? If the door should open, what do you do? You work-off of everything that is dished up to you.

Look, if you have the only set of keys to your car and you are inside your home eating dinner and suddenly you hear the car's engine start, you are going to have some very specific response to that. And if, as you are running toward the door, you hear the tires squealing on the pavement, well, you are going to have a specific response to that. And when you open the door and see that it is actually your neighbor's car being stolen, you will have another very specific response to that, and so on. *ok I'm getting it now...*

If you really watch and listen, you will see many actors only act *yes* when they are talking. When they are not talking, they are wait- *:)* ing for their next opportunity to do some more great talking. *cool* But acting is not about picking up the cues, we must continually be in response to what is happening. What makes us say the lines are our impulses to respond, and these come from our availability to everything that is coming our way!

*To the Observer: Make sure the person with the activity does not give up doing it to have casual conversation with their partner or to play the good hostess or for any other reason unless something that they get from their partner makes them give up the activity. If they are giving up the activity for no good reason, you can say "Don't give up what you must accomplish," or "Don't drop the activity." The exercise can be longer now, a good ten minutes or so. When you decide to stop the exercise depends on what is happening with the partners who are working.

Go ahead now, do some work, each person doing one exercise as the partner inside with the activity and one time outside, coming to the door. As before, do not end the exercise until the Observer tells you it's over. Then read on.

· · · · · · · ·

Let's talk now about the next step in building the activity and get very clear on what your homework will be for Session Ten. To do that, I have a question for you and I want you to write down three possible solutions. Taking the activity that you brought in with you today, *out of your imagination*, what might be a *simple and specific* reason you are in your room doing this very difficult task?

In your notebook, I want you all to write down three different possible reasons for your activity. Simple and specific! Do that now and then read on.

· · · · · · · ·

The activity holds within it the essential elements you will put to use in every acting demand you are asked to realize! As you create the activity, there are key questions you must ask yourself over and over again. You will begin to learn how to talk to yourself as an actor. You will expand and deepen your actor's imagination.

To help you along this path, with each new step we take in "building the exercise", I will give you an invented example of an exercise in the format of a "conversation" between myself and the "students" who just "worked." (Each "conversation" will be a *new pair* of invented students.) Listen especially to the questions that I ask, as they will lead you toward a way of speaking to yourself *as an actor*. Let's get to the next step in the work with the following example:

Conversation In Preparation For Your Next Exercise

EXERCISE

- One person has an activity that is simple and specific.
- The other person comes to the door, knocks three times and enters.

1) To the student with the activity:

Larry: What was the activity?
Student: I was trying to make an origami bird.
Larry: Was it any origami bird?
Student: No, it was an origami eagle.
Larry: Great! That's specific. Not any bird, an eagle. And what is that other piece of paper you have with you.
Student: These are the directions on how to make an origami eagle.
Larry: Good, that was very difficult for you to do.
Student: Yeah, I've never done origami before!
Larry: Also, you weren't doing an eagle from your head, you

were doing that specific eagle on the instruction page. That way you really know when you have accomplished what you are setting out to do. Now, what was the simple and specific imaginary reason that got you to stay at home and make this origami eagle today?

Student: There is a competition.

Larry: OK, there's an origami competition. So, why are you entering it?

Student: Just to win the respect of my friends.

Larry: First of all, take out the word "just", it's never to "just" do anything! You know, that reason sounds complex to me and general. How do you really know when you've got the "respect of your friends" and which friends? This is your first time giving the activity a reason, so let's work it through together. Let's get very simple here. Why else might you be entering?

Student: There's a prize.

Larry: Good, what is it.

Student: A lot of money.

Larry: That would be nice but you know what, a "lot of money" is general. Even if it were ten thousand dollars, it's still general. Ten thousand would also be nice but until you know specifically what you *absolutely* have to have the money for, it is general. Let's stay away from money for the moment, we'll talk more about it some other time. Let's get real simple. How about this prize, what would you just love to win in a contest today? What would really turn you on?

Student: A new car.

Larry: Yeah? What car?

Student: A Toyota.

Larry: What Toyota is your dream car? I mean you're the one making up the prize, why not make it fantastic!

Student: The Toyota pickup.

Larry: Ahh, a Toyota pickup!

Student: Four-wheel drive!

Larry: What color?

Student: RED!

Larry: A red, four-wheel drive, Toyota pickup. That's simple and specific. Isn't it now more important to you that you get the eagle perfect and win the contest? Also, isn't it more specific to say a red Toyota, four-wheel drive pickup than to say "to win a new car?"

Student: Yeah.

Larry: Specific to whom?

Student: To me.

Larry: That's right and that's what counts. OK, let's practice some more. Out of your imagination, what is another possible simple and specific reason for making the origami eagle.

Student: I'm going to give it as a gift.

Larry: That's a good start. Who are you going to give it to?

Student: A friend...I know, that's general—make it more specific... no, not a friend, to my mother.

Larry: Does your mother like origami? Or eagles?

Student: Well, she's not really into origami or eagles, but she goes wild over anything that I make myself, by hand. Like last year for her birthday, I made her this little stained glass box and she went nuts! When I was in elementary school, every wall in our old house was covered with my drawings.

Larry: Great! Now that's a reason that turns you on. As you talked, your eyes were glowing. So again, the reason is?

Student: I'm making an origami eagle to give to my mother as a gift.

Larry: That's a simple reason and for you, extremely specific! Terrific! Getting back to today's exercise, I want to say something about your working-off of your partner. Were you at all aware that she was absolutely fascinated with the origami that you were doing?

Student: I did notice that she was watching me with these warm eagle eyes of hers. *(he laughs)*

Larry: Why do you laugh?

Student: Because I just said "eagle eyes" and, you know, I was making an origami eagle. It's just so cool that I would describe her with that phrase, I guess there's something with me and eagles...

Larry: So you were aware of her behavior. Listen, you must work from that awareness. What might you have said to her?

Student: I could have told her that she was really attentive.

Larry: Right, or even, "You've got those eagle eyes on me!" You see? How did you feel to be watched in that way?

Student: A little self-conscious but, ummm, mostly I liked it, I don't know...

Larry: Yes, you do know. Take your time...

Student: Well actually, I felt so appreciated.

Larry: You felt appreciated! Isn't that great? Listen, our emotions have no reason, they are not "reasonable," they just are. "Why does this little thing make me feel so much?" There are no "little things". Who knows why some things impact us in tremendous ways. Of course we could spend years getting to the root of each reaction—that is not the process we are involved in here. In our work together, you never have to explain or figure out why you feel a certain way, you simply feel that way. We must *embrace* exactly what is happening, work from it and not try to make it more or less than it is.

Student: This is embarrassing, but at one point I really wanted to give her a hug.

Larry: Then, in that moment, what must you do?

Student: Give her a hug?

Larry: *Why not?* Let your impulses lead you, as you begin to let go of "The Internal Censor" you will discover a whole new world available to you in this work.

2) To the student who came to the door:

Larry: You know, there was a lovely shift in your work today. Very relaxed and unforced. You took in your partner fully and you simply worked-off what he gave to you. You didn't try to find the things to work-off and you didn't push to make something happen. You accepted and were available to what was happening. I must tell you, that simplicity and honesty, the way you really listened to him, was magnificent to witness. I mean that! How often do we sit through plays and keep hoping there will be just one authentic moment, one moment of living human contact. But don't get me started on that. What was your experience today, how did it feel for you?

Student: This was a first for me. This felt so different. Up until now, I have been so frustrated. Like I was never gonna get it! Every time I would leave here or finish working with my partner between sessions, I would get very depressed. I started to think that I was inept and that I should give it all up.

Larry: And you kept doing the work.

Student: Yes....I did. And this time it wasn't so hard, it was actually fun!

Larry: Good, from today's experience you learned something of lasting value. And who did it? You did! Look, I can only lead you in a certain direction but it was your commitment and hard work that made today's breakthrough possible for you. Of course, the danger now is in trying to have today's exercise when you do your next exercise.

Keep up the work everyone, see you next time.

• • • • • • • •

So you see, in the sessions ahead, you are going to get deeply in touch with what *really means something to you*. That's what you work from as an actor, always. The process of the activities is exciting work and tremendously rigorous. Be ruthless with yourself and the payoff will be great! (That means, DO YOUR HOMEWORK!)

Now I want you to go back and look at your three reasons for your own activity and see how you did in the areas of simplicity and specificity. Then if needed, rework your reasons until you feel satisfied that they are as simple and specific as you can get them. When you've got it, write down in a one sentence statement, the activity and why you are doing it. (Just as in the "Student's final statement in the Example: I'm making an origami eagle to give to my mother as a gift.") Remember, because of this reason, you would be driven to accomplish this task.

One other thing. The activity you brought in today may have been, in a way (like the balancing of the stick we did) mostly a game. Maybe yours was something like pitching pennies into a bottle, or tossing playing cards into a hat, or spinning a basketball on a finger. These are all fine for today but you know, they are like bar games and other than to win a bet, pretty hard to really justify. (We'll talk more about this in the homework assignment...) Go back into your notebook now and do what you can with today's activity and then come back and read on.

• • • • • • • •

HOMEWORK

For Session Ten, you must have an activity that is physically difficult to do, the more difficult to do the better. There must be a simple and specific reason that you are doing it and it must be a genuine task (not a bar game!). You must always bring with you whatever you need to complete that genuine task.

So what is a genuine task? Simply, it's something you would really do for the reason you've given yourself to do it. This does not mean something that you would normally do.

What is normal?

For example:

You may hate to draw pictures and so you never do it, BUT TODAY is your little sister's birthday and she loves two things— Disney's *Beauty and the Beast* and puzzles. So, you bring with you a set of colored markers, the videotape of *Beauty and the Beast* (it has a great picture on the cover) and one of those pre-cut puzzle cards that you can write or draw on and then take apart for someone else to put together. Your activity is to *draw a picture of Beauty and the Beast on the puzzle card to give as a birthday card to your little sister.* (The videotape will be the gift!)

So you see, in the normal course of events, you would never spend your time drawing a picture of *Beauty and the Beast,* BUT TODAY you are excited to do so because you can just imagine how happy your sister will be when she puts the pieces of the puzzle card together. Got that?

Good, now get to work! And keep up the repetition between Sessions, as often as you can. (Not with activities. You do those at your group meetings.) See you at Session Ten!

Oh, the power of working well, the feeling of power that races through your veins and heart! Oh, the deep content of sitting in the creative climate! In that warmth there is no longing, no yearning, no loneliness or unhappiness. One functions and the self is forgotten, although it is the self most alive and quivering. It is joy, no other word.

—Clifford Odets
from *The Time Is Ripe,*
The 1940 Journal of Clifford Odets

Building The Excercise

Ready to work? Good, everyone has their activity, yes? Again, the activity must be physically difficult and must have a simple and specific reason that you are doing it. Let's get into the exercises.

The exercise today is set up in the same way as we did it in Session Nine. Before we begin, let's review:

• Partner A is in their room with the activity and Partner B is coming to the door.

Note to Partner A: when you go into your room, sit for a few moments and review, in your mind, what your activity is and why you are doing it. Then, GET TO WORK!

Note to Partner B: remember to give your Partner a good couple of minutes to get involved in the activity before you come to the door.

- Partner B will knock three times in different ways.
- Partner A will describe the knocks out loud.
- On the third knock, Partner B will enter and repetition begins. Off you go!

Also, let me bring back into your awareness two keys to the work:

I. *"Don't do anything unless something makes you do it."*
II. *"The quality of your acting depends on how fully you do what you are doing."*

So, do you have a good reason to do the activity you brought in today?

THEN DO IT!

REALLY DO IT AND GET IT DONE!

DO IT BECAUSE *YOU KNOW WHY!*

And don't give it up unless something makes you do something else!

Whatever you are doing, do it fully!

To the Observer: A friend once described to me what he thought made an effective football coach. He talked about a professional quarterback who, in a very intense championship game, was throwing a lot of passes but not getting the ball to the receivers. A time-out was called and the quarterback walked to the sideline and was approached by the coach. My friend said that the quarterback never took his eyes off the field and remained silent, listening intently, as the coach said only a very few quiet words. The quarterback then walked back onto the field and play soon resumed. In the first play back, the quarterback completed a pass and in rapid-fire succession, he completed pass after pass, quickly moving his team toward the goal line. The coach was able to "see" something from where he was that the quarterback wasn't seeing. With his brief words, the coach was able to help the quarterback be more available to what was happening on the field.

More and more now, your job is to be continuously working-off, (from where you are sitting), both of the partners who are in the exercise. You must actually become the "third partner." When necessary, you must jump in and: 1) coach the partner with the activity to Really Do It and not give it up unless something Really Makes Them give it up, and 2) help bring the partners into closer, moment-to-moment contact and a greater availability to "what's happening" by pointing out moments they are missing or responses they are not expressing.

Very important here, you must keep the partners in the repetition. They will often, at this point, stop doing it just because that seems "more natural" to them. THIS ISN'T NATURAL! It's an exercise and you must help them stay in there with each other by yelling in, "DON'T DROP THE REPETITION!" or simply, "REPEAT!" The repetition simply must become habitual. You help them now, OK? Of course, ultimately, I don't care if, in the exercise, neither partner says a word for ten minutes—WHEN SOMETHING MAKES THAT HAPPEN! You are both absolutely silent—not because YOU WANT TO BE but because YOU HAVE TO BE, BECAUSE OF WHAT YOU JUST GOT FROM YOUR PART-NER AND WHAT THAT DID TO YOU! LOOK, IT IS NOT ABOUT THE WORDS AND IT IS NOT ABOUT THIS REP-ETITION BUSINESS OR ANYTHING TO DO WITH TECH-NIQUE—IT IS ABOUT TWO HUMAN BEINGS FULLY AVAILABLE TO EACH OTHER, RIGHT NOW! Is that confusing, when I have just told you not to drop the repetition? It's like a big mental maze, isn't it. That's OK, hang in there...

...and listen, now that I told you all that, don't try to do it, right? ...Remember?... Simply keep doing the things you are learning to do and at some point, it will all do you!

After each exercise, I want the person with the activity to tell the group what they were doing and why. Then, as a group, led by the Observer, I want you to discuss:

1) Did the person with the activity make a consistent and real attempt to accomplish it?

2) Was the activity physically difficult and could it have been set up in a way that would have made it more difficult, yet not impossible?

3) Was the activity set up in such a way that the person doing it knew specifically what they had to accomplish and when it would actually be complete?

4) Was the reason for doing the activity simple and specific? Could it have been more specific?

OK, get to work. Have each person do one exercise as the person in the room with the activity and one as the person coming to the door. This means that everyone will get to do their activity today. After each exercise, have the discussion I have just outlined in the Observer notes. Then read on.

• • • • • • • •

From now on, at each Session after the group has completed doing the exercises and having the discussions, I want you all to take some time to write in your journals. Write about your own experience in doing the exercise, responses to how your activity worked for you, what you got out of the discussion that followed your exercise and what you learned from witnessing and discussing the other exercises in your group.

Also, I want you to know that I am available to assist you in your process. You will find information in my biography at the beginning of the book on how to reach me with your questions.

So, go ahead now and take whatever time you need to write in your journals and when the whole group has finished, read on.

• • • • • • • •

We must move forward now and add the next element in building the exercise. The exercise you prepare for our next meeting, Session Eleven, will have all the components we have worked on so far, with one addition: The reason for doing the activity is now A LITTLE MORE IMPORTANT.

Now before I get into today's sample exercise, take out your journals again and write down two different ways the reason you had for your activity today would be a little more important. Then read on.

• • • • • • • •

So the activity must be physically difficult, the more difficult the better. And the reason you give yourself to do the activity is specific and, rather than simple, is now a *little more important.* (...And the reason comes from where? From your imagination!)

Conversation In Preparation For Your Next Exercise

THE EXERCISE

• One person has an activity that is "a little more important."
• The other person comes to the door and knocks.

1) To the student with the activity:

Larry: What was the activity?

Student: Cleaning and polishing this pair of shoes.

Larry: Why?

Student: Because I borrowed them from my best friend. They're her favorite shoes and I got them kind of dirty and I have to return them to her.

Larry: This thing you say you had to do—polishing the shoes—well, you never really did that. Look at the shoes, are they ready to give back to your friend?

Student: No, not really. They're still pretty dirty.

Larry: You know, when you first began the exercise, before you let your partner in, it was very clear that cleaning the shoes had some meaning for you. Is your best friend really important to you?

Student: Yes, very.

Larry: How do you think she would react if she saw her shoes in this condition?

Student: She'd be very disappointed in me, being so careless with them. She's meticulous with her clothes. I'd feel awful that I let her down.

Larry: By the way, are those shoes actually your friends favorite shoes?

Student: No, I took a pair of her old shoes that she said I could do whatever I want with and in my own mind, I made up that these were her favorite pair.

Larry: FANTASTIC! That's using your actor's imagination! And how did they actually get dirty?

Student: I walked around in a sandbox at the park so I could use them for this activity.

Larry: Good. And I love that you went the extra length and used a pair of her shoes rather than just any shoes, that's great! We'll talk more about that in a future session.

Student: But boy is she ever a neatness nut, that's for real! Is that OK, I mean, that's not using my imagination.

Larry: Not only is it OK, it's absolutely right on. Your girlfriend *is* really important to you, she has real meaning to you and you really know something about her fastidious nature. Very good, that gives you something real to work from, that makes you actually want to fix the mess you made. Then you don't have to pretend to want to do this (and wow us with some clever acting). YOU DO WANT TO DO THIS! You see?

Student: Yeah, I think I do. When I was in the sandbox, I don't know, just thinking about the shoes... maybe it's silly, they're just a pair of shoes but I felt like I was, in some way, ruining our relationship—you know, the trust—I mean, we've known each other since we were ten... well I really started to get upset...

Larry: I like very much what I'm hearing. I will get very specific about this, "the element of truth," in Session Eleven. And, did you really borrow and mess up your best friend's *favorite shoes?* No, you made that up out of your imagination. You created that reason out of your imagination based on an element of truth, which is its importance to you. In this case, how you feel about your friend. Terrific! Hold on to that one! I do want to get back to the other aspect of how the exercise just went, that you never did what you had to do, you never really cleaned the shoes. There are two main issues here. First, as soon as your partner came in, you gave up what you were doing. You played the good hostess, (the nice routine) when what you really wanted to do was clean the shoes. Even though I yelled in *"Get Done What You Have To Get Done, Because You Know Why!,"* you never really did it.

Student: That's true, I felt awkward when he came in, just letting him stand there, you know, just ignoring him while I did the shoes. And you know Larry, I also felt afraid that if I put all of my attention on my activity, I would not be available to my partner. That I would not be able to work-off of him.

Larry: That's a wonderful awareness! You just raised the unanswered question we introduced back in Session Seven, when we began work on the activities: "How do I do my activity fully and also work-off my partner fully?"

Oh boy, this is a great question! You see the exercise is: *"I must do this (my activity) but then there's this (my partner)."* There is an inherent conflict here, isn't there. Two things are pulling at me at the same time. And as the exercise continues to grow, those two pulls will become quite intense!

"How do I do This (the activity) when there's This (my partner)." The answer is: "YOU MUST! AND OFF YOU GO!" Do you hear that? "YOU MUST AND OFF YOU GO!" Off you go into the rollercoaster of moment-to-moment working-off where anything is possible. You might be thinking that I haven't really answered the question. The only worthwhile answer will come when you have the experience in the exercise of fully leaving yourself alone—when you are no longer trying to be available, you are available!

I can tell you that what you ended up doing here was half doing the activity and half working-off of your partner, *so both suffered.* What must you be doing?

Student: Whatever I do, do it fully.

Larry: Right, 100 percent, and that means if you have to get something done, get it done and don't do anything else unless something really makes you do something else. And if your partner makes you do something else, do that 100 percent—until something makes you do something else.

Look, let me interject something here. When you are on stage, what do you look at? How do you know where to place your focus? WHAT GARBAGE! FOCUS, SHMOCUS! If you're worried about what to be looking at, where to be focusing, you're out of the ballgame. But do you know how many actors worry about this or what to do with their hands, and so on? When you are leaving yourself alone, your eyes look at what grabs their attention, your hands do exactly what they must. If you were walking down the street with your girl-friend and a man comes up to you, raises a large wood stick and begins to thrust it rapidly toward your face, I bet that your hands would respond immediately and appropriately. I also bet, in that moment, that you'd be much more interested in keeping your face in one piece than in impressing your girlfriend!

So, I said two issues. The second is that the reason you gave yourself to do the activity was not yet a *"little more important."* It's really still at the "simple" reason stage. Now it must be a little more important, specifically. Let's say your friend needed the shoes back because she's going out on a very important date tonight—This guy might be "THE ONE"— and she wants to wear these shoes with her new dress. Now, isn't it a little more important that you get the shoes back into great shape before she picks them up? And isn't it more specific than "You just have to return them to her?" Yes it is. And, who knows it's a little more important? *YOU DO!* Also, the actual physical difficulty of the activity itself wasn't set up specifically enough. Can you see that?

Student: Well, I guess it wasn't all that physically difficult. I mean, it was mostly just getting all the sand out of them and polishing up the outside.

Larry: Right, it was generally getting them cleaned up. Can you think of a way to make the same basic activity more difficult to do.

Student: Well, hmmm... what if I got some paint on one of the shoes?

Larry: Now you're talking! Even if it's one good spot of paint, now it's much more difficult to get that shoe looking like new and now, you've really got to work at it. And isn't it more specific to clean off this one large spot of paint than to just "clean up a pair of dirty shoes?"

Student: Yes and that also gives me a bigger challenge.

Larry: As you set up the activity, you must keep asking yourself the important questions: "Can I make this more Specific?"

"Can I Make It More Physically Difficult?" Ask until you are satisfied that you have taken it as far as you can.

2) To student who came to door:

Larry: I want to ask you about something and I believe this is crucially important for your own process of growing through this work we are doing together here. Are you aware that from the time your partner opened the door until the moment I stopped the exercise, you were smiling.

Student: Well, I'm not aware it was constant, no.

Larry: I'm telling you that it was. The smile never left your face. The main thing is that you really didn't find anything funny. Actually, after a short while of being in the room, what I got out here, is that you became quite bored. Is that true?

Student: Well, when she sat down with those shoes, I felt like there really was no reason for me to be here, I mean I just wasn't interested in what she was doing.

Larry: That's OK, but that wasn't OK with you.

Student: I thought I should be encouraging.

Larry: The Magic Word! You *thought,* thinking! You know, your thinking will continually get you into trouble. If you are thinking, where is your attention?

Student: …On myself?

Larry: Exactly! And where must it be?

Student: On my partner.

Larry: Right. So you and your partner had a lot in common here, a common ailment, you were both "putting up with each other," in other words, playing Mr. and Mrs. Nice Guy.

Student: Is there something wrong with being nice to her?

Larry: Nothing is ever wrong when that's what's happening! If it is true, that you really want to be nice, be so nice that you make her feel like a million bucks! Great! But it wasn't, you were bored to tears and it was painful for you to sit there and have such an empty conversation.

Student: That's true. So I really should have expressed that.

Larry: Well, what could you have said to her?

Student: I guess I could have said, "This doesn't interest me," or "You are boring me"…God, that's direct!

Larry: You just shocked yourself, didn't you. That's very new and uncomfortable for you. YES IT IS DIRECT! You don't know yet that that is really OK. I'm telling you that not only is it OK, and I've said this before, it is a gift to your partner and to yourself. You get to be the full expression of who you truly are in this moment, to LIVE FULLY RIGHT NOW! (And getting out of your own way, is living!) Your partner now knows exactly where you stand and she has something REAL to respond to! Astounding! What we are talking about here is absolutely awesome, I promise you, it is awesome.

What I'm pointing you to is "the we, we don't know." Most of our lives we live in "the we, we know." We have made all these decisions about ourselves—what we believe in, how we should behave, what we can handle, and so on. Thus we operate in "the we, we know" and we are in control. But acting, at least the kind of acting we are interested in here, demands a giving up of that control, a turning ourselves over and allowing a possibility to discover "the we, we don't know." If you asked Mrs. Smith, who weighs 112 pounds, as she is walking along Maple Street with her son Billy if she can lift a car, she ("the she, she knows") would laugh and say, "Don't be silly, of course not." Then suddenly you hear a blasting of horns and a tremendous screech and there is Billy, under the tire of a pickup truck. In that moment, Mrs. Smith discovers herself lifting the truck off of Billy's chest, she discovers "the she, she didn't know."

I'll say one last thing about this for now. You know, we live our lives as if "we know" and I am telling you, we don't know. As much as we would like to think that we do, WE JUST DON'T KNOW. You stand waiting in line at the cafeteria thinking, "Corned beef on rye… yummmmmm, corned beef on rye… I gotta have a corned beef on rye… Oh boy!

Corned beef on rye…" Suddenly it's your turn, the lady says "Whatta ya have!" and out of your mouth comes, "Tuna on whole wheat."

Now, I really shouldn't assume anything here, I should ask first. Do you want to work more authentically even though it may be very uncomfortable for you? Is that what you really want for yourself in your work?

Student: Yes. It does feel scary but I really do want that.

Larry: Great, then let go of the forced smile. It's in the way of where you want to be in your work. Now that you are aware of it, you can do that. It will be a relief, I promise you. Risk saying what you really want to say and see where that takes you. You know what? Your partner can handle it. And take out those pauses of thought from your repetition. This will help you in two ways—in staying in contact with your partner and in leaving yourself alone.

Thank you both for your work today!

• • • • • • • •

HOMEWORK

For next time, everyone bring in an activity that is physically difficult to do—Specifically!—and has a reason that is a "little more important" to you—Specifically!

Look folks, the key is in *being specific*, it is always the way in. It's the only way in. Everything in your set up of the exercise, must be specific. Anything left general will result in general acting. So, just like we had all over the walls at the Neighborhood Playhouse, put up a big signs over your desk, your bed, on your refrigerator, in the bathroom—"BE SPECIFIC!"

As for repetition, this is the last time I'm going to say this, keep on practicing it whenever you can, throughout all of our sessions together. Be well my friends, see you at Session Eleven!

*S*urely all art is the result of having been in danger, of having gone through an experience all the way to the end, to where no one can go any further.

—Rainer Maria Rilke

In The Extreme

Purr

Let's go. In a moment we'll get into the exercises you have pre-pared for today. To review, the elements in the exercise as it is set up right now are: One person is in the room and one person is coming to the door. The partner in the room has an activity that is physically difficult and has a reason to do it that is "a little more important."

As of today, we will no longer be using the "three knocks and enter" ingredient of the exercise. So that's over, right? Beginning today and from now on, we return to *the door is always locked* (review "coming to the door" in Session Six.) So the person who comes to the door simply comes to the door and knocks. The person in the room will respond to the knock however they do and off you go. That's that, simple, right?

Once again, everyone will do two exercises. One as the person in the room with the activity and one coming to the door.

To the Observer: One comment. Now that the person in the room will be opening the door, be attentive to if that partner gets stuck in "casual conversation" at the door when what they want to do and need to do is "GET DONE WHAT THEY HAVE TO GET DONE, BECAUSE THEY KNOW WHY!" And of course, that's what you can say when that happens. Help them give up the nice act and complete what they know they must accomplish, the activity.

And to repeat from our last session, (I will not review these questions in this way after today) after each exercise, I want the person with the activity to tell the group what they were doing and why. Then, as a group, again—led by the Observer—I want you to discuss:

1) How was the working-off? Were there any specific moments that either partner didn't work-off or respond to?

2) Did the person with the activity make a consistent and real attempt to accomplish it?

3) Was the activity physically difficult and could it have been set up in a way that would have made it more difficult, yet not impossible?

4) Was the activity set up in such a way that the person doing it knew specifically what they had to accomplish and when it would actually be complete?

5) Was the reason for doing the activity specific and "a little more important?" Did it have real meaning to the person doing it. Could it have been more specific?

Finally, after all of the work and the discussions, take the time you need to write all of your thoughts, feelings, and experiences of today's Session in your journal. Please do not skip over this important part of the process.

OK, ready? Good, get to work! After the exercises, the discussions and the journal work, read on.

• • • • • • • •

FOR OUR NEXT SESSION

In the last Session, I promised you that I would get more specific about this thing called the *"element of truth"* in the reasons for your activities. I will now address that as well as other essential aspects of the activity. We must also move forward and add some new elements to the building of the exercise.

So we have gone from an activity that had no reason, to one with a simple and specific reason, to one that was a little more important. For the next Session and from now on, the activity is set up *in the extreme*. It must be "extremely meaningful." Extremely meaningful to whom? Yes, to you. *well*

The activity must be set up in the extreme. It is no longer "a little more important," it is now VERY IMPORTANT! It is VITAL! CRUCIAL! URGENT! THAT YOU GET IT DONE! What we are doing here is raising the stakes. The stakes must be very high and there must be no way out except by completing this most difficult thing that you have come home to do.

So, the reason might be that:

"If I can accomplish this, get this done right now, the outcome would be _____!"

Or, "What has just happened is _____!"

Or, "What I have just found out is _____!"

Those blanks must be filled in with words such as: "The

Greatest!" "The Most Exciting!" "The Best In My Life!" "The Most Exhilarating!" "The Most Joyous!" "The Most Wonderful!" And so on.

If we say to ourselves:

"If I do not accomplish this, right now, the outcome would be _____!"

Or, "What has just happened is _____!"

Or, "What I have just found out is _____!"

Those blanks must be filled in with words such as: "The Worst!" "The Most Horrendous!" "The Most Dreadful!" "Catastrophic!" "The Most Devastating!" "The Most Terrifying!" "The Most Humiliating!" And so forth. *ok motive*

How you talk to yourself is vital:

It is not, "kind of nice." It is,
"THE MOST FABULOUS AND FANTASTIC!"

It is not, "pretty lousy."
It is, "THE MOST DISASTROUS!"

stakes!

Do you see the difference? I do mean in the extreme! So, how do we get there? We must begin to develop a specific way of fantasizing, of daydreaming. A deepening of our "actor's imagination." But you know, usually, most of us only permit ourselves to go so far in our fantasies and no further. When we get to the place where it becomes, "Too terrible to imagine!" or "Too fantastic to hope for!" we do not continue. *Now, we must!* We must go on into where it is dangerous to tread, we must go that far. We must allow ourselves to fantasize without inhibition, to imagine the unimaginable, think the unthinkable. Listen, you know you are on to something with your reason for the activity when it gets uncomfortable to even think about. And this doesn't only apply when you are thinking in the direction of "dire" consequences. It might be as uncomfortable for you to imagine how thrilling it would be to have a "dream of a life come true!" Which ever direction you take it, you must make the activity as extremely meaningful as you can. Specifically! Specifically!

Let me give you an example:

Let's say that Sharon is doing the activity. Her activity is embroidering a very specific butterfly design, one that has had special meaning to her daughter, onto the daughter's favorite sweater. The reason she is doing this is because she wants her daughter, who has just been killed by a hit-and-run driver, to wear it when she is buried today. *woah*

Now look, this is uncomfortable. I know it is, I'm sitting here at this computer and I am shaking. It is horrifying to imagine and if you are a parent, I know you know. You may say, now that's going too far, I don't want to go that far, and I am telling you that you must. I'm not saying to use that reason, those circumstances may have no meaning for you. I am telling you that whatever reasons you do come up with, they must be that extreme.

This brings us back to the "element of truth" which is the activity's importance to you. In Sharon's case, the element of truth is her relationship with her daughter. It's the bottom line. This is something she really knows. It lives in her and is absolute. And this is what fuels Sharon's activity. And as Sharon begins to fully accept the imaginary circumstance, what she "really knows" is what makes her hands tremble so violently that it is nearly impossible to do the needlework. Sharon is also very wise in helping herself deepen the reality of this exercise by using one of her daughter's actual favorite sweaters and deciding to embroider a butterfly, which her daughter loves. The imaginary part of her setup was that her daughter was killed by a hit-and-run driver and that the funeral is later today.

Let me show you how Sharon could have used the same basic setup, with just a few changes, to go in a very different direction with this activity:

She is still doing the butterfly needlework but now, the daughter, has spent the last three weeks in the hospital after being struck by a hit-and-run driver (one of the weeks in a coma). The daughter has had a miraculous recovery and Sharon will be bringing her home today. Sharon is preparing the sweater as a wonderful surprise for her daughter to wear on the trip home.

I'll tell you something else. Out of the meaning Sharon's daughter has to her, this very specific "element of truth," she can create from it an endless variety of imaginary circumstances, of extremely meaningful activities. Listen, when you have hooked into something that is so powerful and vital to you, YOU'VE STRUCK GOLD! So as you struggle to create the activity, you are mining for gold, gold that is rich in personal meaning. And hey, how many gold mines do you really need?

The activity is a product of your imagination based on an element of truth, which is its importance to you.

You may have noticed that I said Sharon "accepted" the imaginary circumstance. I did not say that she "believed" them, acting is not believing (Does the actor playing Hamlet "believe" he is talking to the ghost of his father?) it is accepting. It is fully accepting the imaginary circumstances and living them out as if

accept ≠ believe

they are true. That's Actor's Faith, THAT'S ACTING! And the way in is:

1) The activity must be physically difficult, the more difficult the better.

2) The activity must be extremely meaningful. To whom? To You!

3) In every aspect, BE SPECIFIC! Anything left general, will result in general acting.

As in the "Sharon" example, something I have found true for myself and very useful for the students I have taught, is that the reasons you create for the activities, the "imaginary circumstances," will work on you with greater potency, will find deeper roots, if they are not about yourself but are mainly about or specifically include someone else. Someone who has great meaning to you.

Here is the setup for your next exercise which you will bring into Session Twelve. One person is in the room with the activity. Again, the activity is physically difficult and now extremely meaningful. The other person is coming to the door—with one addition:

The person coming to the door now must have a simple and specific reason that brings them to the door.

Let's talk about this. Up until now, as the person coming to the door, you had no idea what was bringing you there. All you knew was that I had told you to come to the door and knock. Now you do know why you are coming. It is a simple and specific reason that gets you to come and knock on the door, right now. Remember, simple and specific. Let's say you are coming to borrow a cup of sugar. That's simple and specific. An important question is, now that you have this reason, what do you do about it? Your partner opens the door and you've come to borrow a cup of sugar, what do you do about that? Take a moment to write down your answer in your notebook and then read on.

. . . .

If you said "Try to get the sugar," "Ask for it," or any other form of "Play my objective," well listen, that's not what this exercise is about. Remember this one, "Don't do anything unless something makes you do it?" So, now that you know why you are coming, what do you do about it? Don't do anything about it, KNOW IT! Know it and see what happens. Work-off your partner and see where that takes you. (Sandy told us, "It's not about what you show, it's about what you know!")

That you came to get a cup of sugar may never come up. I mean, who knows what you will be entering into when that door opens? Your partner may be in the middle of a seance and about to get some crucial advice for his new magic act from Houdini. Do you think you would interrupt that for some lousy sugar? Of course, it is also possible that as the door opens, your partner might pull you into the room, push you up against the wall, shake you and scream, "WHY ARE YOU HERE BUGGING ME!!" Well the appropriate response might be, "TO GET SOME SUGAR, PAL!!"

What I am telling you is, now you know what brings you to the door. It is simple and specific. Unless something makes you, don't do anything about it, *Know It.*

Conversation In Preparation For Your Next Exercise

EXERCISE

- One person has an activity that is extremely meaningful.
- The other person has a simple and specific reason that brings her or him to the door.

1) To the student with the activity:

Larry: What was the activity?

Student: I got fired, so I was filling out an application for a new waiter job and to get the job, I have to hand the application back in by five o'clock today.

Larry: So why is it so important to get this job today?

Student: Oh, it's really important for me to have this job because, uh, two reasons. One, I'm about three thousand dollars in debt, I've got about two hundred dollars in the bank and, uh, the rent's due on the fifteenth and my girlfriend has no work right now. So, and she's the one that I owe the money to, so on top of all that, she loaned me all of her savings for me to study at the University and I have no money to pay her back or pay the rent and she hasn't the money either so it's extremely important that I get this job.

Larry: Yeah? Why?

Student: Why? *(He laughs...)* If I don't have this job, I don't have a place to live and I can't even honor my debt to her.

Larry: So... she'll be upset...

Student: She'll be upset and it will put our relationship under even more stress.

Larry: Why won't you have a place to live?

Student: Well, my landlord doesn't exactly take kindly to us not paying our rent.

Larry: So...

Student: So we'll be out on the street and there's a good chance he's gonna be extremely pissed off.

Larry: Will you be out on the street or do you have other places...

Student: Well, we're new in this town and I've established no real close friendships.

Larry: So you might have to move back and live with a relative or...

Student: Well actually I hadn't even considered what the options would be, I'm just thinking about this job, that's my only option.

Larry: No, it's not your only option. I mean there are options. Rather than be on the street, there are probably some other people—relatives, friends somewhere that might take you in.

Student: Yeah, yeah there are other people I guess but...

Larry: Or is it possible that, knowing your situation was desperate, a relative or a friend might lend you a couple of months rent until you got back on your feet?

Student: Yeah, uh well, that would be possible but...

Larry: No, no buts, is it POSSIBLE, that's what I'm asking, is it possible?

Student: No it's not possible seeing as they wouldn't even loan me the money for the class I'm taking, let alone my living expenses...

Larry: What I'm asking is, honestly, if you called up your best friend or closest relative and said, "We are going to be on the street in two days!" is there a possibility that somebody would send you the rent money?

Student: ...It's possible, yeah.

Larry: It's possible. OK. I'm leading to something. IT'S POSSIBLE! And at this point, your reason for the activity (which wasn't really physically difficult) was general and not really in the extreme. First, and I may have said this before, the problem with using money to drive your activity is, unless you make it very specific, money is general. I don't care if you are winning a million dollars, money on its own doesn't mean anything. Yes, I know you had to pay the rent and the loan but listen, we all have to pay the rent. It's tough but we do it.

Those reasons, though important to everyday survival, are pedestrian, do you see? They are ordinary and not tied to our fantasy life. They do not spring out of our greatest dreams and desires, our inner world of "wish fulfillment!" or from our most horrific fears of dreaded consequences! The other main thing is, and the reason I kept pushing you with the "is it possible" thing, is that when you are building the reason for the activity, you want to paint yourself into a corner. You must put yourself in a situation where there is no way out. There is no way out! There is no possibility except by doing this impossibly difficult thing you have come home to do, right now! It must be, "I MUST DO THIS RIGHT NOW BECAUSE I HAVE NO OTHER OPTIONS!" It must be that extreme.

Student: Well I thought about this element of truth thing and for the most part, the entire circumstances I used, are true.

Larry: You got fired and you're looking for a job?

Student: Well, this is a real job application for a real job and there is a real deadline, and I really am in debt and the subject of getting fired just came up at my job and so there's a lot of truth to this...

Larry: Theatre is not an imitation of life, it demands a greater truth. The same with this exercise, it is not an imitation of your life.

Student: What about this "element of truth" thing?

Larry: Doing your taxes is important and is a difficult task. If you brought in your taxes as the activity today and today is April 14th, it is certainly urgent that you get them done but it is not a good activity. It is not yet a product of your actor's imagination, it is merely a chore dictated by the reality of your life. Do not confuse that with "the element of truth." Let's take another look at your activity. Let's take one part of the reason you gave which is that you have this girlfriend. You took all of her savings and because of you, you may both lose your apartment. Now maybe she has a lot of meaning to you. Does she?

Student: Oh yeah.

Larry: OK, so there's the part that you might really want to get into. Your girlfriend has great meaning to you and you are letting her down in a big way, well that's the element of truth. Say you begin there, "I took all of her savings and spent it on myself," and you continue fantasizing, "We don't have health insurance and she just found out that she needs this very crucial surgical procedure. The doctor said that he will not report anything until we are on an insurance plan but he said make it fast because she must take care of this. If we quickly get married and I get the job, I'll have a health insurance plan for the two of us, so I JUST GOTTA GET THIS JOB, TODAY!" That's a quick idea for you, but now we have an element of truth, which is her real meaning to you, "I love this woman, I took all of her money, what the hell am I doing!"

Student: Yeah, right, this is good.

Larry: So then out of your imagination, well you take it from there, but it now becomes truly urgent and very meaningful because her life is on the line and there is no way out, "We just have to get the insurance, there is nobody who can give us that kind of money, there could be complications, who knows what!" Now, the money becomes specific. Now, it's not about the money, it's that you see the woman you love standing in front of you, she's deathly ill and you've only made her life more difficult. Uncomfortable to think about?

Student: Oh, extremely uncomfortable!

Larry: That's when you know you are on to something. Now, because the activity didn't have any real meaning to you, it became easy to give up—which is why you never completed the application. How far did you get on it?

Student: Uh, not very far...

Larry: If it had meant something to you, you would have done it with an unrelenting commitment. And when it was finished, you would have shot out of here like lightning, running off to that restaurant, making sure that you got the job. As it was, you gave your partner most of your attention (and there was nothing very pressing in her behavior to make you do that).

Student: Yeah, I see that now. And, I do see, well, as you talked about my girlfriend getting ill, I mean, I do feel very guilty about taking all of her savings to use for my classes. The truth is, she sacrificed a lot to help me out. She even gave up something, well, she put on hold something she had been waiting a long time to do with her money. I mean it was a dream of hers, I feel really lousy about it... *(He begins to cry.)*

Larry: *(There's a long pause.)* Now listen, you must work from this place of deeper meaning within yourself, it has to be that personal. As you talked, you discovered the source of some great activities. Hey, what if, out of some wonderful surprise event in your life, you were suddenly able to give to her the very thing she put on hold when she allowed you to pursue your studies. How would that make you feel?

Student: Fantastic. That doesn't even describe it, uh, joyous, triumphant, Yeah, triumphant!

Larry: Well, there's another direction to take yourself. Now create a physically difficult activity that you will be compelled to do out of that extremely meaningful reason.

Student: It is so hard coming up with the activity part, I mean, the reason is so difficult and then making the two work together and being very specific, I…, well I'm having a tough time—this is hard.

Larry: It Is Hard! Do you think it would be of any value if it was a breeze to do? It is rigorous work and it never gets easy and it is always uncomfortable. That's theatre. That's theatre when you are after the real thing. You know, there is a price to pay, if you want the real thing there is a very high personal cost — but you know what? The rewards are great!

You know, I used this term before, "wish fulfillment." That's a great place to start when fantasizing about your activities. Let's say that you know that your girlfriend loves calligraphy and though you have never done it before, you are learning to use a calligraphy pen. You are preparing to inscribe one of her favorite poems on the inside of a card in the most beautiful penmanship. At the end of the poem you are going to add, as if it were part of the poem, your own words of love and your "Triumphant news" that you are giving back to her, her "life's dream!" The one she had put on hold, because of you.

Listen, the possibilities are infinite. You must really get into the world of your imagination, of wish fulfillment, in the extreme. And you must ask yourself and grapple with the main question, "What really means something, TO ME!"

2) To the student who came to the door:

Larry: What brought you to your partner's door today?
Student: I wanted to borrow his car to go grocery shopping.
Larry: Good, simple, and specific. Also, your working-off was fine. He was extremely casual and relaxed with you and you responded to that just fine.
Student: There didn't seem like there was very much to do so I sat down and enjoyed his company.
Larry: There's really not much to say. You took what you got and didn't try to make it anything else. That's great, keep going in that direction. You wanna go buy your groceries now?
Student: Well, if class is over...
Larry: Class dismissed!

• • • • • • • •

SOME NOTES

I want to give you a few important pointers on activities and exercises before we wrap up Session Eleven.

1) Do real things and be who you actually are.

Set up the activity so that you are able to do real things. So that you are not pretending to do it, you are actually doing it. If you cannot figure out how to do your activity with real things, then it is not a good activity.

This is different than using an object and giving it a specific meaning out of your imagination. You can get an old plate from the Salvation Army store, break it into a hundred pieces and say that it was precious to your mother because it had belonged to her grandmother. When you begin to put the plate back together and as you accept the imaginary circumstances, the plate will become personally meaningful to you.

But if your activity was to announce over the air waves, during your radio show, a secret coded message to save your son who is being held by kidnappers... First of all, the exercise is always in your room and you are always who you are. Don't pretend to be a radio personality with a pretend microphone talking to a pretend radio audience.

Or this famous exercise:

Student: You see Larry, in this exercise I am a cowboy and it is vital that I perfect my lasso tricks for the upcoming rodeo!
Larry: Why are you suddenly talking with that funny accent and walking like John Wayne?
Student: Well I'm a cowboy and it is vital that...
Larry: Where are you from?

Student: Hoboken, New Jersey...

Larry: Are you really a cowboy?

Student: Well, no, but I always wanted to be one and...

Larry: Great, then set it up so that YOU are practicing the lasso tricks so that YOU get to be "Cowboy for a day!!" in Hoboken's first annual "City Slicker's Rodeo."

This also applies to who your partner is to you. You know exactly what you know about your partner and their relationship to you is whatever it actually is—no more and no less. So if you are working with Sally, a good friend, when you open the door and it's Sally, who is she to you? Right, she is your good friend Sally. Simple, right?

One last thing, when you set up a reason about or including someone else, it must be based on what is true for you about that person, *today*. For example, if your activity is making an invitation to send to family members for a special 80th birthday party for your grandfather and what is true is that your grandfather is no longer living, then this is not a workable set- up for the exercise. But if you chose that activity, you probably have deep feelings for your grandfather, so set it up in another way. You could be doing the same activity but now you are inviting all the family members to a very special event you are hosting, celebrating your grandfather's life. Asking everyone to bring and share their wonderful memories about him! *interesting*

2) Do not do illegal or personally harmful things.

I'm not going to tell you how to live your life but I am going to tell you something about a life in the theatre. We never drink real alcohol on stage so don't do it in the exercise. (And since we don't pretend, well you can see that "getting drunk" is not a good activity.) It is illegal to do drugs—they have no place in our work and they have no place in the theatre. The theatre, as well as any place that you are doing "the work," is a *sacred space*, please treat it as such.

Smoking a Mark

Also, please don't do activities that could seriously harm your partner or yourself. So no getting ready for the big knife throwing event tonight, OK? Or practicing for the practical section of the "body piercing" board exams?

This reminds me of another important point. The exercise can become quite explosive. Of course, you do not want to censor yourself and I do not want to inhibit you in any way—*AND*—it is important *never to harm your partner.*

Now there is nothing wrong with some real physicality between the two of you but please grab his shoulders instead of yanking on his hair. And if your partner makes you so mad that you want to kick in his face, kick the couch instead. If you want to throw him across the room, throw a chair instead. You see, you must be fully expressive and you must not harm your partner! I have seen partners hurt each other very badly in acting exercises, you must get that THIS IS NOT OK.

Of course, accidents may happen but you must have, *at all times,* a little voice in the back of your head that knows how far to go and when to redirect your energy so that your partner and you are safe. Please, this is crucial! There are actors without that little voice, I call them "oblivious actors." There is just no excuse to say, "Well, I was just so 'into it' that I broke his arm." I will not work with an oblivious actor and I hope you won't either. Enough said.

• • • • • • • •

HOMEWORK

Get to work and prepare your exercise for Session Twelve. To review:

- One person has a physically difficult activity that is extremely meaningful and in every nook and cranny—SPECIFIC!
- The other person has a simple and specific reason that brings him or her to the door.
- Also, at this point, I want each set of partners (whether your group has three people or twenty-three) to do only one exercise at each meeting.

This means that I am asking you to have two work meetings for each of the remaining Sessions in the book.

At the first work meeting for the Session, one person in each partnership has the activity and one comes to the door. At the next work meeting, the partners switch and you have a totally new exercise set up with all of the elements we are currently working with. Got that? Only then do you move on to the next Session in the workbook.

By the way, do you remember when we first began activities and you were balancing the stick? If you think back, you will recall that I said to, "Do it as if your life depends on it!" Remember? Well at the time, that was completely general, wasn't it. "What does he mean like my life depends on it, I'm just balancing this stupid stick!" There really was no reason in the world to do it as if your life depended on it. NOW THERE IS, AND YOU MUST KNOW WHY. SPECIFICALLY! Now, get to work. See you next time.

Theatre is a safe place to do the unsafe things that need to be done. When it's not a safe place, it's abusive to actors and audiences alike. When its safety is used to protect cowards masquerading as heroes, it's a boring travesty. An actor who is truly heroic reveals the divine that passes through him, that aspect of himself that he does not own and cannot control. The control and the artistry of the heroic actor is in service to his soul.

We live in an era of enormous cynicism. Do not be fooled.

Don't act for money. You'll start to feel dead and bitter.

Don't act for glory. You'll start to feel dead, fat and fearful.

We live in an era of enormous cynicism. Do not be fooled.

You can't avoid the pitfalls. There are lies you must tell. But experience the lie. See it as something dead and unconnected you clutch. And let it go.

Act from the depth of your feeling imagination. Act for celebration, for search, for grieving, for worship, to express that desolate sensation of wandering through the howling wilderness. Don't worry about Art. Do these things and it will be Art.

—From the *"Authors Note"* to *The Big Funk*
by John Patrick Shanley

Taking It Personally

In the remaining Sessions, I will not be guiding you through the "work" portion of your meeting. I trust that by now, as a group, you have developed a way of being with each other and of working with each other. I know that you will do the exercises, the discussions, and the journal work. At that point, you may proceed into the preparations for your next meeting.

So gather around gang, come on, get those hands into the middle of the circle. Are you all up for this one, huh? Come on, I can't hear you! I said ARE YOU UP FOR THIS ONE!! That's better! Now I want you to get in there and do the work! And listen to these words from your coach who loves ya!:

If you have the impulse to do something, DO IT!

If you have the impulse to say something, SAY IT!

Do not hold anything back!

Should you take what your partner says and does personally?

Did you hear the question? Should you take it personally? What's that? I can't hear you!

"Well, I don't have to take it personally, I mean she really didn't mean to..."

BALONEY!! SHE DID MEAN IT SO IT IS PERSONAL! IT'S ALL PERSONAL! YOU MUST TAKE IT PERSONALLY!

OK! And you there, yeah, you with the activity. Fight for your life and get it done, right? Right! AND WORK-OFF EACH OTHER! OK, That's it, give it your all, play your hearts out and have a great time! OK, READYYYYYYY...WORK!!!! (Excuse my humor but we must stay lighthearted. Making it all too self-important will create another constriction of our acting instrument. So work now and then read on.)

· · · · · · · ·

As I told you in Session Eleven, you will repeat today's exercise before moving forward into the assignment for Session Thirteen. After this work, you may read on.

· · · · · · · ·

FOR OUR NEXT SESSION

We will be adding two elements to the exercise that you will prepare for SessionThirteen. For the person with the activity, I now want you to add "Urgency." Urgency is a specific time limit. You only have "this much time, specifically" to complete the activity. Up until now the activity was generally urgent, you knew you had to get it done right away. *Now it must be specifically urgent.*

How do you determine the amount of time you should give yourself? Decide what you think a reasonable amount of time would be to do the activity and then cut it down so that it becomes extremely difficult! Of course, do not make it impossible, that would defeat the purpose here. For example: If the activity is putting together a 1000 piece puzzle, you wouldn't want to say that you have only thirty seconds to complete it. That would give you nothing to really fight for. But if you thought it would normally take two hours to do, you might decide that you only have forty-five minutes to get it done.

One important note. The activity must still be extremely physically difficult on its own. You cannot rely only on the urgency to make it a challenge. Teamed up with the physical difficulty, the specific time limit now makes the activity even More Difficult! And that's exactly what you want to do for yourself, make it more difficult!

The other element we are adding is for the person coming to the door. Last time, you came with a simple and specific reason. Now, it must be "a little more important." Not extreme, *a little more important.* So, last time, you came to borrow the car to go grocery shopping. Great, that was simple and specific. Now, it's a little more important. So now, you are coming to borrow the car to go grocery shopping because "This very special guy is coming over for dinner tonight and he loves spaghetti with spaghetti sauce and I'm all out!" Now going grocery shopping is a little more important to you. It's not extremely important, I mean if worse came to worse, he'd probably settle for your meatloaf and potatoes. But you would sure love to serve him that spaghetti!

• • • • • • •

Conversation In Preparation For Your Next Exercise

EXERCISE

- One person has an activity which is physically difficult, that is extremely meaningful, and which has a specific urgency.
- The other person has a reason that is a little more important which brings him or her to the door.

1) To the student with the activity:

Larry: What was the activity?
Student: I'm building a model house out of toothpicks.
Larry: Why?
Student: My wife went to our doctor this morning before going to work because she thought she was ill. She's been in meetings so I haven't been able to reach her on the phone. So I called the doctors office to see what happened because my wife didn't call me to tell let me know what the doctor said. The nurse got on the phone and said, "Congratulations!" and then told me that my wife is pregnant.
Larry: Clearly, that was extremely meaningful for you.
Student: Something surprising and amazing happened to me when I was coming up with this activity. I was thinking about my wife and that she has been talking a lot about how empty she feels inside, well, about not having a child. And that her whole life is her job and that she doesn't even feel connected to it anymore, except in getting the paycheck every week. And I'm the one who keeps saying to her that there is no way we are ready, either financially or emotionally, to have a baby. That we need more time to be alone, just her and I, and that we need to get more solid on our feet... Anyway, I woke up in the middle of the night the other night, so I went into the living room and started to fantasize about this whole thing and I kept seeing how sad her eyes have gotten, like a deadness in

them. That really hurt... Then I started to think about having a baby together, about saying to her, "Yes honey, I want to do this with you and I want you to be happy again." And then I saw her eyes come to life, they were bright and alive, like they were when we first met and that made me feel so terrific. I got so caught up in the fantasy, I wanted to scream! I mean, I just kept seeing her eyes alive again and I thought, well, I would do anything in the world to have them look like that.

Larry: Fantastic! You are really making the process your own and in a powerful way. Also, by fantasizing so freely you were led to something very important to you. That you discovered the look in your wife's eyes and their deep meaning to you, now THAT'S SPECIFIC! Do you all see that? And thank you for sharing with us so personally and so honestly, it helps all of us go further in our own work. Now, how did that look in her eyes, that "element of truth," lead you to the toothpick house?

Student: Well, we had this old joke that someday we would have a baby and a dog and we would buy a piece of land in the mountains and build a log cabin there. That we would be a log cabin couple with a log cabin baby and live a log cabin life. So, I'm making a model of our log cabin life with toothpicks and I'm going to surprise her with it. I'm going to mount it on this *(He pulls out a big sheet of cardboard.)* and draw pictures of mountains around the house, with little streams, you know.

Larry: Great. And tell me, what are the smaller objects you made, the ones you put inside the house—will you show them to us?

Student: *(He takes four small objects out of the model house, also made from the toothpicks and holds each one up for us to see)* This is my wife, this one is me, this is a dog and this one is a crib for the baby. There's also this one that I haven't finished yet, it's the baby.

Larry: This is great work! It was also urgent for you to do and you worked on it with a passionate fervor. I also like that you held on to the reality of that time limit. I even saw you checking your watch every so often.

Student: I set up the urgency so that I was going to bring the log cabin to my wife's office and leave it on her desk for her to discover when she comes back from lunch. I know she gets back to work at 1:15 and it takes me twenty minutes to get to her office. That gave me only an hour to finish the whole project. I don't know if this other part is okay but I decided that I was going to hide in her supplies closet, which is right across from her desk and when she picks up the "log cabin baby," I'm going to jump out and take a photo of her with my camera.

Larry: Why wouldn't that be okay?

Student: I thought it might be getting too carried away, making some kind of complex plotline.

Larry: Listen, it's only an empty plotline when it has no meaning to you. It has to *turn you on to do.* It has to live in your gut and in your heart. It must possess you, because it means that much. Which this whole activity does, in a big way for you. So it's not just okay, it's terrific. By the way, where is the camera?

Student: *(He reaches into a bag and takes out a polaroid.)* Right here.

Larry: Good. Does it have film in it?

Student: Yes, I put some in when I was preparing all the things I needed for the activity.

Larry: Now that's the reality of doing! Now I'm really getting excited! Let me tell you all something. He could have made his life a lot easier if he had decided that because the camera really wouldn't have to come out during the exercise, he just wouldn't bring one. None of us in class would have known, right? And that's what most actors do on the stage. And I do mean most so-called professional, working actors! They don't pay the price, they don't go all the way. They come from an attitude of "Why bother, the audience won't know anyway" and that's why most theatre today is an empty vacuum.

That your classmate here did bring the camera and that he did load it with film, now that's working like AN ACTOR! That's going all the way! And he doesn't do it for us, he does it for himself, for the deepening of his own experience of living out the imaginary circumstances "as if" they are true.

And by the way, I want you all to hear this, isn't it possible that today his wife just might take the afternoon off? *Is it possible?* Isn't it possible that his wife might walk in the door right as the toothpick cabin is just about finished? It's possible, right? Well now, he can pull out that camera and take the photo of her right here in the living room. You see? Fantastic, absolutely fantastic! (Know what else is fantastic? Do you remember what he did when he heard the knock? He hid the whole log cabin activity, he put it all away before he answered the door! "Maybe she lost her keys!" Now that's living truthfully in the imaginary circumstances. That's living, not just doing an exercise.) Now, is it okay if we use your camera to take a snapshot?

Student: Sure.

Larry: Bonnie, quick, take a picture of your Partner so he can show his wife that glowing face of his from this exercise he just did. *(Bonnie takes the camera and shoots a picture of her Partner, who is now ecstatic.)* You know, your work with your Partner was also the best it has been for you. You were continually in response to her and you were going fully with where you were being taken. You really turned yourself over to both the activity and to your partner, I bet that felt great!

Student: Yeah, this whole thing was a gas!

Larry: You know, that activity is still living in you, isn't it. When the activity really takes root, it's hard to just drop, we can't, it lives in us for a while. That's working for real.

Student: You know, I want to go home and have a baby right now!

Larry: Better get your wife to take the afternoon off!

2) To the student who came to the door:

Larry: What brought you to the door?

Student: I really needed a thesaurus so that I could finish writing this article I've been writing that I just found out had a real good chance of being published.

Larry: Very nice. What is the article about?

Student: It's a kind of personal diary of living with food allergies.

Larry: And who's thinking of publishing it?

Student: *The New York Times.*

Larry: Hey, good for you! Let me tell you something, your work today was quite beautiful. That reason had a specific meaning to you and it lived in you in a way that was out of your control. And the best part of all is that, once you came into the room, whatever was happening, you were able to go with it instantly and fully. You were truly living in the present, in a moment-to-moment responsiveness with your Partner. In order to highlight what I'm talking about, I want to point out a few specific moments.

When your Partner opened the door, we saw a huge smile on your face and your arms raised triumphantly in the air. Now the immediate connection between the two of you and what you both had going on, resulted in your partner lifting you off the ground, swinging you around and screaming. You suddenly found yourself screaming and laughing and dancing with him. What an absolutely fabulous moment for both of you!

Student: Yeah, that totally took me by surprise. It was great!

Larry: You then spent quite a long time in awe of his beautiful cabin creation as you became both his cheerleader and his ally as he struggled to get the job accomplished.

Student: I was really fascinated by the way he was working so delicately and precisely.

Larry: And then, at a certain point, the reason that brought you here, erupted back into your consciousness. Listen, you learned something crucial today. When you make the reason strong, you don't need to hold on to the meaning, it holds on to you!

Student: Yeah, I really forgot all about my article for a while, and the thesaurus. I was so into what he was doing.

Larry: But then you began to get very uncomfortable just standing around watching him. He worked-off that very nicely, he said, "You need something, don't you?"

Student: I wanted to still be happy for him but when I realized that I gotta get back to my writing, I just didn't want to waste any more time. I even got angry that I was wasting time.

Larry: Right. And when he kept saying, "Then get what you need already! Get what you need!" You yelled, "I need a thesaurus!! You got one???" That was right on, you said that because your partner made you say that. When he yelled back at you, "No, I don't," you yelled "DAMN!" and you ran out of the room.

Student: Well, when he said that he didn't have one, I knew that I better go to the store or something. Go somewhere else and get one.

Larry: Absolutely! There was no reason to stay, so go! Listen, all of you, don't ever stick around just to do some more repetition or just to keep the exercise going. If something really makes you want to leave, go. Then when you go, see what that does to you and work from that.

Student: When I got outside the room I was afraid that I had abandoned him in the exercise.

Larry: Hey, you gave him a great moment! When you left and slammed the door, he threw a toothpick at you and yelled, "Too bad, Toots!"

Student: *(She roars in laughter.)* "Toots?"

Larry: We all had the same reaction. Great work you two. Thanks!

• • • • • • • •

HOMEWORK

So it's back to work and setting up your next exercise.

- One person has an activity which is physically difficult, that is extremely meaningful, and which has a specific urgency.
- The other person has a reason that is a little more important which brings him or her to the door.

Got it? Good, see you at our next meeting.

building up little by little

Your attempts to answer the question, "What must I do?" may lead you to embrace and study both philosophy and technique; to learn to meditate and to learn to act, so that your personality and your work become one, and you fulfill your true purpose, your highest purpose, as a member of the theater.

—David Mamet
from *Writing in Restaurants*

S e s s i o n   T h i r t e e n

In Relationship

I want to give you a way to begin the exercises from now on.
Both partners will leave "the room" and, as you go out, you will
leave the door open. Both of you will go to separate places and
take some time to fantasize about, daydream about, free-associ-
ate about the reason that you have given yourself. You do this
until the reason starts to "do something to you." When it does,
you know that you are ready to begin.

In this way, I want you to start grappling with what you must
do to prepare yourself to begin, because you must never begin
"cold," in other words, you must never come from nothing. And
that's as specific as I will get about what you do out there to
ready yourself. (I will not be dealing with the next major part of
the Meisner process, "Emotional preparation," in this book. It is
something, I believe, I can only work on with you in person.)

So, for the person with the activity, when you are ready, come in, close the door, and get to work. For the other person, whenever you are ready, come to the door and knock. (If the door is still open, you know your partner is not in the room yet, so go away and keep fantasizing. At some point, come back again.)

As we have established, you will have two meetings for the current exercise before moving forward. Don't rush the work! I believe, at this point, it would be counterproductive for anyone to prepare and work on two exercises at one meeting.

So, have two good work meetings and then read on for the new elements in the setup of the exercise.

· · · · · · · ·

FOR OUR NEXT SESSION

I am going to give you two new elements for next time. One for the person coming to the door and another for the both of you to create together. Other than these, the setup for next time will contain all of the elements which made up our previous exercise. We are building something here, we're building!

First, and I bet this will be no surprise to you, the person coming to the door will now have a reason that is "in the extreme." At first it was simple and specific, then it was a little more important and now, it must be *extremely meaningful*. A good approach to coming up with this reason is thinking of it in this way: It is something you have *just* found out or that has *just* happened that is extremely meaningful to you. And then you come to the door!

Some pointers:

A) Your reason must have nothing to do with your partner who is in the room. What I mean is, you have just found something out or something has just happened that is extremely meaningful to you and it does not involve your partner.

B) You are not coming to get anything or to do anything, you are coming from this thing just happening or from just finding something out that is in the extreme—TO YOU! Please do not worry about why you are coming to the door. Work on making the reason as specific and extremely meaningful to you as you can and then come to the door and knock.

C) So this meaningful thing has just happened or you have just found it out. So what do you do about it when you come to the room? *You know it,* right? You *don't do anything,* know it and *see how it does you.* Again, if it is living in you, it will have an impact on you that will be out of your control. That's what you want and that's what you work from. You work from exactly what is happening. You wanna scream, scream! (And work- off your partner.) You wanna cry, cry! (And work-off your partner.) You wanna kick off your shoes and dance around the room, do it! (And work-off your partner.) And, if your reason just didn't do much for you today, what must you do, always? Yes, WORK-OFF YOUR PARTNER!

D) As in the reason for the person with the activity, this reason must also be out of your imagination based on an element of truth, which is its importance to you.

E) Finally, the JUST in "just found out" or "just happened" is crucial. It didn't happen last week and you didn't find out yesterday. It JUST HAPPENED! Or, you JUST FOUND OUT! and that brings you to the door.

Examples:

• Your sister, who is also your best friend in the world and lives in another city, was told by her family doctor that she had breast cancer. She went to a second doctor, a specialist, for tests. You just found out that SHE IS PERFECTLY FINE. THERE IS NO TRACE OF CANCER! and then you come to the door and knock.

• Your cousin, who is the only remaining family that you have, was coming on an airplane to visit you. Earlier in the day, you heard a radio newsflash that the airplane lost an engine and crashed over the Atlantic Ocean. The airline office said there would be no use in going to the airport and that they would call you with any updates. *The call just came* and you found out that there are no survivors! And then you come to the door and knock.

Second, I am now going to add something that will be new for the two of you. We will now add "relationship." Up until now, in the exercise, the two of you were exactly who you are to each other. Now, I want the two of you, together, to decide on a simple and specific relationship for yourselves. It can be any relationship as long as, in the relationship, you do not live together. Here are some examples: neighbors, co-workers, sisters, cousins, classmates, you're on the same bowling team, fiancées, you're in the church choir together, and so forth.

Some pointers:

A) Here's the old trick question again, now that you have a relationship, what do you do about it? THAT'S RIGHT! YOU KNOW IT! What is there to do about it? Should you both behave like people in that kind of relationship are supposed to behave? Listen, there really is no such thing as "relationship."

Relationships are defined by what is happening "right now," in the present. Relationships are a living thing. You see, many actors determine that this is "a mother-daughter" play and proceed to act the way "all" mothers and daughters behave. Isn't that ridiculous? Is there any one kind of mother-daughter relationship? Is there one kind of any relationship? Of course not! There are mothers and daughters who adore and respect each other and are the best of friends and there are mothers and daughters who are the fiercest, meanest and most back-stabbing rivals. Isn't this true?

B) And so, there is no need to make the relationship more "real" by giving yourselves some kind of "history" together. You work-off each other, moment-to-moment, coming from all the meaning you have built into the reasons for being there, and you will see a real relationship come to life on you! We must stay away from the cliché of relationship—and working with each other, in the present, is how. You know, when you are living in the moment, there are no clichés! Let's get to the example exercise.

Conversation In Preparation For Your Next Exercise

EXERCISE

- One person has an activity that is extremely meaningful, physically difficult, and which has a specific urgency.
- The other person comes to the door from something he or she has just found out or that has just happened that is extremely meaningful.
- The partners have a simple and specific relationship.

1) To the student with the activity:

Larry: OK, wait a minute here, I have to stop the exercise. Let's talk about this. What are you doing? What is the activity?

Student: *(He is out of breath.)*I'm looking for the keys to my car and I can't find them anywhere!

Larry: Well you certainly ran around a lot but you never really looked for the keys.

Student: But I was looking!

Larry: No, you were running around. By the way, in setting this exercise up, how did you make sure the keys would be hard to find?

Student: Well, I left them on my chair in class. I didn't bring them into the exercise so that I'd have a really difficult time finding them in my room.

Larry: You mean, so that you could pretend to have a difficult time finding them.

Student: I don't get that, pretend!

Larry: Well, if you really know that they are on your chair in class and not in your "room," what's there to really look for? Remember, I've said that in the exercise, we never pretend to do anything. Now if you had asked one of your classmates to hide your keys in the room for you, when you went out to get ready, wouldn't you then have something to really look for? As it was, I could name a dozen places in the room that, in the whole ten minutes, you never fully searched.

Student: I'm telling you I really looked! Look, I worked hard on this idea, I worked all damn week! Aren't you going to ask me why I'm looking for the keys?

Larry: Go ahead.

Student: I just found out that my fiancée has decided that she won't marry me and that she is on her way to the airport where she's going to take a plane to Italy. I knew that I had four minutes to find the keys or I could never get to the airport in time to talk her out of backing out of the wedding on me. That's extreme!

Larry: I stopped the exercise after about ten minutes and you were still in the room.

Student: I had to find the keys!

Larry: COME ON NOW, COME ON! WHAT ABOUT THE GIRL! THE WEDDING! THAT PLANE TO ITALY! If that reason had the meaning you say it has, brother, come four minutes you would have bolted out of here and you'd be *on your way to the airport*—if it meant grabbing a cab, hitch-hiking or hijacking a bus! You would have done everything and anything humanly possible to get there before that plane took off!

Student: Look, you don't know what this means to me, you can't read my mind!

Larry: It was all in your behavior.

Student: Look "Mr Zen," you can stuff your behavior!

Larry: It's a lot easier for you to make this about me. You know, I've been very patient with you but I'll tell you something, your overwhelming need to "be right" is what's engulfing you and killing all possibility for you to get anything out of this work. And I won't continue with you in this way.

Student: *(He stands up and screams.)* NO, I WON'T CONTINUE WITH YOU! *(He walks out of the classroom.)*

Larry: *(Turning to the class.)* Now if he could bring some of that to the setup of an exercise, look out!

   I'll tell you a true story. When I was thirteen, we got a call, very early in the morning, from my grandmother. This was in the middle of one of New York's all-time biggest snow storms. My mother had picked up the phone and Grandma told her that my grandfather, my father's father, had just died. I remember, within the next minute, my father had thrown on some clothes and a coat and he shot out of the front door and into the storm! I watched from the dining room window as he trekked past the car, which was totally submerged in the snow, and made his way to the corner. Late in the afternoon, we got a call from my father. He told us that he had walked to the highway and he had finally stopped one of the very few cars that were on the roads—a car which was traveling in the opposite direction!—and that he actually talked the driver into taking him all the way to my grandparents' home. What was normally an hour drive, was on this day, an almost six-hour drive. I heard that my uncle, who lived farther away, was trying to hire a helicopter!

Well, let's move on...

2) To the student who came to the door:

Larry: I never got to ask your partner, what was your relationship?
Student: We were ex-lovers.
Larry: And what brought you to the door?
Student: It had to do with something I just found out about my father, but it didn't really work for me...
Larry: What did you find out?
Student: I found out that he was very ill.
Larry: Yes?
Student: Well, that's it, that's what I found out.
Larry: At this point, the reason is still general. *(The student is looking down at her lap and she has become very still. After a long pause.)* You're very upset. *(She remains very quiet.)* Would you be willing to talk through this together?
Student: Yes, I want to.
Larry: Tell me more about the reason.
Student: Well, I knew that it was general. I mean, I really wanted to set up a reason about my father and when I was fantasizing, I started to think about him getting sick and then I couldn't go any further.
Larry: It was scary.
Student: Very scary. When I was at home, just thinking about it made me cry and cry. But I was really afraid to let myself get any more specific than that.
Larry: Can you talk more about that fear?
Student: I was afraid to think about him in that way.

Larry: Afraid in the sense of having your thoughts about him come true? Like, you might make something really bad happen to him by thinking it?

Student: Yes, you know, that is exactly what I am afraid of. I may be superstitious but that's why I have only been able to use "happy" type reasons in the exercises so far. But I feel like there's this whole other part of me that I'm cutting off. So this time, I really wanted to explore in a new direction.

Larry: That's great and this is a wonderful awareness. And, I don't think it's as simple as superstition. I think, in one way or another, we all have to deal with feelings that come up when we are putting our closest family members and our best friends into all kinds of extreme circumstances, even though it is in our imagination. For myself, I have found that doing so has always gotten me more deeply in touch with how much I love them. I know for many students, it is the belief that thoughts, put out into the universe, create reality. I wouldn't argue with that *and,* I do believe that it is one's intention that is most important. I think we must get real clear on the answer to this question: "For what purpose am I sitting here in my room, in the dark, having all these terrifying thoughts?"

Everything you are doing here is in the pursuit of learning a craft, growing as an artist, and doing so with the highest integrity. *(As my friend, the playwright Arthur Giron, once told me, "Hold tight to your integrity! You'll be a radiant beacon of light in a very dark world.")* Why bother? So that through your acting, you will heal the planet. Which is what real theatre does. Because a real theatre springs only from love. Coming from that place, I believe you can explore within yourself freely, without fear, because the universe knows and understands your purpose. This may all sound a little too "New Age" or "spiritual" for you, or you may find it very useful. (And, by the way, in all of my years of working this way as an actor, none of the "bad" things I have fantasized about have ever come true.)

Student: Personally, that all helps me, it helps a lot. I hadn't thought about it in that way before. Anyway, yes, that helps very much.

Larry: Good, do you want to continue, see if we can take today's reason a little further, make it more specific together?

Student: Yes, I'd like to do that now.

Larry: So tell me about you and your father.

Student: We live at opposite ends of the country, so we don't see each other too often. When we talk, he doesn't always really listen to me and I don't think that he really knows who I am, which is mostly my fault because it's hard for me to really tell him how I feel inside. But I do know that, definitely, I mean the world to him. He has always and continually been there for me, really, in quite amazing ways. I mean, everywhere I ever moved in my life, from college dorm's to apartments to houses all over the place, he'd be there with a borrowed truck and one of those dolly-wheel things. He was like a one-man moving company! Then, one time, I had started my own business and he would work with me in the evenings, after he worked all day at his own job, as my assistant! And he did it for no other reason than to help me get the business off the ground. And he has always been there to help me when I was struggling financially, always. *(There is a quiet pause...)* I have always wished I could repay him in some way, make his life a little easier, more fun. Especially now... *(Another quiet moment...)*

Larry: Especially now?

Student: Well, the last few years have been very tough on him and my mom, I guess it started with the death of my grandma who had lived with us for many years. She was a special part of our lives, she was like our anchor, you know? Anyway, since then, my dad has had real bad problems with his eyes. Finally he had surgery on one eye, the operation was really botched up, and he lost all vision in that eye. Now, he has a cataract on his other eye, which was always his weaker eye. It's all just so awful...

Larry: You're very concerned about him.

Student: Yes, I am. He came to visit me and my family recently. One day he was sitting in my living room and I saw him from the hallway. He was reading the newspaper, but to read it he had his glasses sitting on top of his head and he had the paper about a half inch from his one eye that can see. I stood and watched as he moved the paper back and forth, back and forth in front of his one weak eye and it killed me. I thought about him having to look at the world that way and it just tore me apart inside. *(She covers her eyes and cries.)* I don't want him to be totally blind. I mean, the blindness would be horrendous enough but I'm really scared about what that would do to him emotionally. *(She is weeping now. The class is silent except for two others who are also crying. No words are spoken for a while)*

Larry: You're very worried about him.

Student: Yes, I am. I think, I don't know, I realized when I saw him like that, although he should be retiring by now, I mean... I know that he still drives to work everyday and at night and my mother told me that every week there's a new little dent on the car and I started to think about him driving off the road one night and killing himself! And there's nothing I can do! I mean the whole thing really stinks...

Larry: You love your father very much.

Student: Yes, I do and, well, DAMN IT! JUST DAMN IT! *(She remains quiet for a while.)*

Larry: Would you like to go and wash the mascara off of your face and blow your nose a little? *(She laughs and the class joins her.)*

Student: Yes, I would love to. *(She goes out to the bathroom. After a few minutes, she comes back in and sits again.)*

Larry: Anything great happen out in the bathroom? *(Everyone laughs again.)*

Student: Well actually, yes, I came up with two really extreme and terrible things I could think about for next time!

Larry: Great! And listen, thank you, thank you so much. I want you to look around the room for a moment. Take a good look at your partners. *(To the class.)* Raise your hand if you want to go home right now and hug somebody or call someone and tell them how much they mean to you. *(The entire group raises their hands.)* Me too!

Listen, you allowed yourself to have a very personal experience here, which we witnessed and which opened us up to our own pain, to our own feelings of brokenness, to our deep desire to have real connection, and also, to how very precious life is. Out of your authentic experience, you enabled us to become more of a true community for each other. And, we are all in this together! You helped us all realize that this is a safe space, that we can be ourselves here, that we can take risks and when we do, all that we get back, is love. And that's theatre, when it's done for real. You know, I could easily tell you how to take what you shared with us today to its most extreme conclusions, but as you said, you handled that in the bathroom!

Student: *(She laughs.)* Yes I did!

Larry: Great. *(He turns back to the class.)* I don't know what will happen with her Partner. He may be gone for good. He's been working up to that anyway. Listen, I do know that this work is not for everyone. It just isn't. As I've said before, there is a high cost, a great personal price to pay. It is now and will always be uncomfortable. And, ultimately, this work leads to JOY! It all becomes JOYOUS! Watch out, living in the present is addictive! GET TO WORK AND SEE YOU ALL NEXT TIME!

• • • • • • • •

HOMEWORK

I know you know but let's review one more time, the exercise for next time:

- One person has an activity that is extremely meaningful, physically difficult, and which has a specific urgency.
- The other person comes to the door from something he or she has just found out or that has just happened that is extremely meaningful.
- The partners have a simple and specific relationship.

Have fun!

The actor must recreate his work, each time he repeats his part, with sincerity, truth and directness. It is only on that condition that he will be able to free his art from mechanical and stereotyped acting, from "tricks" and all forms of artificiality. If he accomplishes this he will have real people and real life all around him on the stage, and living art which has been purified from all debasing elements.

—Constantin Stanislavski
from *An Actor Prepares*

Raise The Stakes

I'm not going to start with a big peptalk. I am simply going to ask you to give it all up today. Let yourself be taken—by the activity and its deep meaning, by the reason that brought you to the door and most of all, by your partner!

You know the setup of the exercise. Have your two work meetings and then read on.

• • • • • • • •

FOR OUR NEXT SESSION

I am now going to give you the next element to build into the exercise. This will be the final setup of the exercise that we will cover in this workbook. It goes like this: Whereas last time the person's reason for coming to the door had nothing to do with the Partner in the room—now, (Can you guess?) that's right, now it does have to do with the person in the room. AND THAT IS WHAT BRINGS YOU HERE! Now it is specifically about or specifically includes your Partner, the other person in the relationship.

Again, it is that: You have just found something out or something has just happened that is extremely meaningful *to you* and it is specifically about or specifically includes the other person in the relationship—your Partner—and then you come to the door and knock!

And listen, you are always coming *directly* to the door. It didn't happen last week or yesterday or two hours ago and then you come to the door, NO, it is that *YOU JUST FOUND OUT AND YOU COME DIRECTLY TO THE DOOR!* It is that *IT JUST HAPPENED AND YOU COME DIRECTLY TO THE DOOR!* (Do you think that I'm trying to stress the importance here?) yeah

Here is an example to make this new element clear. For the structure of the previous exercise, suppose you set it up like this:

Your relationship is classmates. You have just found out that your brother has died due to a drug overdose. And then you come to the door.

In the previous exercise that would have been enough. Now, you could take the same reason and build it in this way:

You just found out that your brother has died due to a drug overdose and *it was your classmate* (Your Partner) who got your brother started on and was supplying him with drugs! And then you come to the door!

Here is an example that doesn't work:

Your relationship is sisters. You have just found out that your sister (your Partner) did not get the "movie role of a life!" that she had auditioned for.

Do you know why that reason isn't a good one? Well, who is it really meaningful to? It may be important to your Partner but where is the element of truth for you? You may fully empathize with her but how is it extremely meaningful to you? Do you get that? Now what if it was *you who lost the part* and you just found out that it was your sister—your Partner—who went and and told a lie to the producer out of which your contract was cancelled. Now come to the door AND KNOCK!

The only other change to the exercise for next time is that *I no longer want you to add urgency to the activity.* The activity remains the same in all other ways but now it does not have a specific time limit.

So to review, the setup for the exercise now is: complex now

• The person in the room has a physically difficult activity, the more difficult the better. The reason for doing it is extremely meaningful to you.
• The person coming to the door has just found something out or something has just happened that is extremely meaningful to you and which is specifically about or specifically includes the other person in the relationship—the Partner. And then you come to the door!
• The partners have a simple and specific relationship.

A pointer: Always work from what you know—no more, no less.

Remember when we talked about point of view? It's what you

know to be true. When you work from that, you can't go wrong. In terms of this next exercise, this reminder will help you handle all situations that may arise. Let's listen to part of an exercise:

There are three loud hammering knocks on the door. Dina is taken by surprise, she drops a section of a ripped up snapshot on the table and runs to open the door. As she opens it, Debbie, who is furious, storms in. Dina gasps in response:

Dina: You are really upset about something!

Dina runs back to the table and resumes taping the photograph back together. Debbie follows:

Debbie: Yes I am upset about something, Dina
Dina: You're taking it out on me.
Debbie: I'm taking it out on you!
Dina: You're really angry at me!
Debbie: Don't play Miss Innocent Dina!
Dina: You're accusing me of something.
Debbie: That's right, I am accusing you of something!
Dina: You're accusing me?
Debbie: Quit pretending you don't know what the hell I'm talking about!
Dina: I don't know what you're talking about!
Debbie: You don't know what I am talking about?
Dina: You are really intruding here Debbie.
Debbie: Too bad you murderer!
Dina: You're calling me a murderer?!?
Debbie: Just quit the innocent act Dina!
Dina: Keep your hands off me!
Debbie: Oh, you don't like it do you!
Dina: No, I don't like it. Quit it!
Debbie: No, I won't quit it you murderer!
Dina: WHAT DID I DO, DEBBIE!!!!

Debbie: YOU KILLED MY CAT!!!!!
Dina: I KILLED YOUR CAT?
Debbie: YOU RAN OVER MY CAT!

Now at this point, Dina has to handle the question of the cat. I have seen students in this kind of situation attempt to "play along" with the partners story. If Dina did that, it would sound something like this:

Debbie: YOU RAN OVER MY CAT!
Dina: Yeah, God I am so sorry. It was a terrible accident and there was a car coming in the other direction and I had to avoid this kid playing ball on the street and I didn't even see your cat run out there but when I screeched to a halt I suddenly saw…

This is a lot of what? PRETEND, right? And we never pretend. Isn't it so much simpler to simply work from what we know to be true? If Dina knows that she didn't kill a cat today, she would sound something like this:

Debbie: YOU RAN OVER MY CAT!
Dina: NO, I DIDN'T! *reverse improv*

Simple, right? Now what if by some strange coincidence, Dina had run over a cat on the very same day as this exercise, then what?

Debbie: YOU RAN OVER MY CAT! *yes and*
Dina: OH MY GOD, THAT WAS YOUR CAT?

Now that's stretching it a little but remember, we must never assume anything, right? The main thing is that, isn't it so much simpler to stick with what you know? Reminds me of an old saying: *"When you don't lie, there's nothing to remember!"*

fun

Here's another thing to consider. Sometimes, when you are in the building stage of the exercise, you may realize you need to tell your partner something that the both of you should know in common. Let's go back to Debbie and Dina, but let's give the climax a new twist:

Debbie: YOU TOTALLED MY NEW CAMARO!!!!
Dina: I TOTALLED YOUR NEW CAMARO????
Debbie: I LENT YOU MY NEW CAR AND YOU WRECKED IT!
Dina: I NEVER BORROWED YOUR STUPID CAR!

You see, Dina handled this moment perfectly, working from her own truthful point of view. But her response really throws Debbie for a loop because Debbie based her whole exercise on Dina borrowing and totalling her new Camaro. *This is where it would have helped if, before the exercise, Debbie had given some information to Dina that they both know in common.* In this case Debbie would have told Dina, "Dina I want you to know that last night, I lent you my new Camaro to drive for a few days." What would Dina do with that information? Nothing, she would hear it, accept it, and forget about it. See, it may never come up, but if it does, you both have a shared truth to work from. Of course Dina still works from what she knows to be true, so now it would sound something like this:

Debbie: YOU TOTALLED MY NEW CAMARO!!!!
Dina: I TOTALLED YOUR NEW CAMARO????
Debbie: I LENT YOU MY NEW CAR AND YOU WRECKED IT!
Dina: I BORROWED YOUR CAR BUT I DIDN'T WRECK IT!
Debbie: You wrecked it!
Dina: "I did not wreck it!
Debbie: You didn't wreck it?

Dina: No, I didn't!!!
Debbie: "Well somebody wrecked it!
Dina: Somebody may have wrecked it but it wasn't me!
Debbie: You really mean that.
Dina: Yes, I do mean it!

In this way, as you saw, Debbie wasn't denied the entire reason she had set up and she got to grapple with a new possibility, "Hey, Dina acknowledges borrowing my car but I really believe her, she really doesn't know how it got smashed up..."

You can also be more protective of your reason when giving your partner shared information. *You can tell them three items of information, with only one having something to do with your reason for the exercise.* In this way you disguise what your reason is about and you keep your partner more in the dark about it. So Debbie might have said: "Dina, I want you to know that you have a dog named Scottie, that you borrowed my new Camaro, and that you bought three tickets to the big seven million dollar lottery today." Dina listens and than forgets about it, if any of those should come up in the exercise, now she knows.

Don't make a big deal about this, have fun with it. It isn't always necessary, so only do it when it is needed. OK? OK! *ok!*

Today, instead of an invented "Conversation," I am going to give you two example exercises to stir up your imaginations as you build your exercises for next time.

EXAMPLE 1

PARTNERS Sharon and Betty
RELATIONSHIP Neighbors
Sharon has the activity.

ACTIVITY Sharon is carving a miniature black bear from a small block of wood.

REASON FOR ACTIVITY

ELEMENT OF TRUTH *Sharon has a very close and loving relationship with her Grandmother Lillie.* Grandma Lillie was separated from her younger brother Jacob, when she was six, right before she came with her mother to America. Although she found out that he went to Argentina with an uncle, she was never able to locate him and has not seen him in seventy-two years. This has always been Grandma Lillie's deepest hurt. She has talked about Jacob with Sharon often, especially a memory of the last time that she was with him. And what stands out most clearly of that moment was that Jacob was eating a green apple and she was holding a little black bear which was carved from wood. *Sharon, for as long as she can remember, has always dreamed of finding Jacob and reuniting him with Grandma Lillie.*

IMAGINARY CIRCUMSTANCE Without telling Grandma Lillie, Sharon hired a team of men who run a private company that specializes in reuniting relatives who have been separated for many years. They have been successful and Jacob was located last week, now living in Texas. Sharon flew him to New York yesterday and got him a room at the Plaza. Tonight, there will be a reunion dinner which many of the family will attend. But first, there will be a private reunion for Grandma Lillie and Jacob, in his room. Sharon is planning to take her to the Plaza, and up to the hallway near his room. At that time she will hand grandma the wooden bear and tell her who is in the room and invite her to knock on the door. When Jacob hears the knock, he will pick up a green apple from a bowl that Sharon put in his room and he will answer the door.
Betty is coming to the door.

REASON FOR COMING TO DOOR

ELEMENT OF TRUTH Betty is madly in love with her husband Nick but they have been arguing a lot and she is feeling unable to break through and open up real communication between them. He has been very withdrawn and defensive. *Betty is very worried about their relationship.*

IMAGINARY CIRCUMSTANCE Betty has just found out from one of Nick's friends who would not keep the secret, that Nick has been having a sexual affair for the past two months with her "neighbor, Sharon!" Betty is coming from this talk with Nick's friend directly to Sharon's door!

(For this exercise, Sharon and Betty would not need to share any additional information. If in the exercise, Betty accused Sharon of being the world's biggest traitor, how would Sharon respond? She works from her truthful point of view, in the moment. Which might sound something like, "I don't know what you're talking about!" or "Betty, you are out of your mind!" and so forth.)

EXAMPLE 2

PARTNERS Lynn and Henry
RELATIONSHIP Co-workers

Lynn has the activity.

ACTIVITY Lynn is learning to sing and play on guitar the Joan Baez song *Recently*. She is using a cassette tape to learn it from.

REASON FOR THE ACTIVITY

ELEMENT OF TRUTH *Lynn has been best friends with Ruth since they were four years old.* Now, twenty years later, they are still the closest of friends and they share an apartment in New York City. They have gone through all of their ups and downs together and they communicate with each other in the most open and authentic way. *They are inseparable!* Ruth has just broken up with her boyfriend of three years and is extremely depressed. She stays in her room by herself a lot, listening to her favorite album *Recently* by her favorite music artist, Joan Baez.

IMAGINARY CIRCUMSTANCE Lynn came home from work two days ago and discovered Ruth in the bathroom. Ruth had committed suicide. The funeral is later today and Ruth's mother has just called Lynn asking if Lynn would choose and sing a song at the service, a song that was special to Ruth.

Henry is coming to the door.

REASON FOR COMING TO THE DOOR

ELEMENT OF TRUTH Henry has been having great financial difficulties and has gone into debt. He has just had his second child and the pressures on him have become tremendous. He is very worried about providing for his family. But he is optimistic because he has been promised a promotion at work which would mean a higher salary and better benefits. He believes the future is bright.

IMAGINARY CIRCUMSTANCE Henry has just come from a special meeting with his boss which Henry was called to even though the offices were closed today. The boss informed him that he was being immediately released from all responsibilities and that he was fired. His boss told him the reason was that Henry's "assistant Lynn" had complained to the boss of Henry's repeated attempts to talk Lynn into having a sexual encounter. Lynn also said that Henry had told her that her future in the company would depend on it. Henry told the boss that it was all lies but the boss said the company could not and would not stand for this kind of controversy in any "way, shape or form!" Henry is coming directly from this meeting to Lynn's door!

(For this exercise, the only additional information I would suggest is that Henry tell Lynn that at work, she is his assistant. Nothing else is needed.)

· · · · · · · · ·

HOMEWORK

Again, you will come back to Session Fifteen and be prepared to do the following exercise:

- The person in the room has a physically difficult activity, the more difficult the better. The reason for doing it is extremely meaningful to you.
- The person coming to the door has just found something out or something has just happened that is extremely meaningful to you and which is specifically about or specifically includes the other person in the relationship (the Partner) and then you come to the door!
- The Partners have a simple and specific relationship.

See you at Session Fifteen.

There is a vitality, a life force, an energy, a quickening,
that is translated through you into action,
and because there is only one of you in all time,
this expression is unique.
And if you block it, it will never exist
through any other medium and will be lost.

—Martha Graham

Doing The Work

Do your work at two meetings and then read on.

• • • • • • • •

As I told you, with this Session we conclude the addition of new elements in the exercise. And that's it for Session Fifteen!

HOMEWORK

I want you to do two more work meetings with the same setup of the exercise from your previous two meetings. Then read on as we "wrap-up" the workbook together! See you there!

There are no shortcuts
when adopting a lifeway
of consequence.

—David K. Reynolds

Wrap-Up!

Having this mind of mine, thoroughly trained to fantasize in the extreme, I thought that I should sum the book up with the most impactful and inspiring words known to man. Words that would leap off the page and make you scream out your window, "I AM AN ACTOR!", or have you fall to the floor, passionately hug this book and weep uncontrollably for days, "YES, YES, I AM AN ACTOR!"

In reality, I know that it will not be any clever words that can do that for you, it will be some profound and unexplainable experience. For me, the first came at the Neighborhood Playhouse, studying with Sandy and my other teachers. Since then, there have been a number of such experiences which have "fanned the flame!" I'd like to share three with you.

One was the performance of John Malkovich in the Steppenwolf production of *True West*, which I saw in New York City while still a young acting student. He embodied not only the values we were learning in our classes but a kind of living on the stage that I was only beginning to imagine was possible. I remember leaving the theatre not knowing what had hit me, hardly able to breathe, dizzy, and leaning against a wall for support. I was that deeply shaken! And at a time when the work in class was tremendously difficult, seeing John Malkovich that night was a loud and clear "YES! YES! KEEP GOING! WHAT YOU ARE DOING IS URGENT, IMPORTANT, AND YOU MUST KEEP GOING!"

Another was a production of *The Three Sisters* performed by the Sovremennik Theatre of Moscow during their visit to Seattle in 1990. Directed by their Artistic Director, Galina Volchek and performed in Russian, this was truly the most awesome event I have ever witnessed in the theatre. A glance, a word, a touch— whatever they did or said, it was filled with the most specific and brilliant life, with the greatest depth of courage, trust, and intimacy I have ever experienced between an ensemble of actors. It was pure love! And when the play ended, I and the entire audience leapt to our feet, cheering for at least twenty minutes as the actors cheered back to us from the stage, in what was much more a group hug then a standing ovation.

The other experience I want to share was actually very similar in respect to the violent intensity of my own physical, emotional, and spiritual response to the work. This time though, it occurred as I read Horton Foote's nine-play masterpiece, *The Orphans' Home Cycle.* I was swept totally into the lives of these complex, surprising, and absolutely real human beings. I fell in love with them and longed to spend more time with them and in their world. I left this experience feeling opened up and more receptive to the gift of humanity all around me, to a call for greater understanding, compassion, and forgiveness. I was reminded that life is so very precious! I completed the plays in awe of Horton's artistic vision, overwhelmed and thrilled by his mastery and simplicity. (By the way, you must read all of Horton's plays! From his very early one-acts right up to the collection, *Four New Plays,* published by Smith and Kraus.)

This reminds me, I wanted to be sure and give you a few titles of books which will support what we have started together. First, you must read Sandy's book, *Sanford Meisner On Acting*, which is the best acting book I know of. I also urge you to buy the book, *Zen In The Art Of Archery* by Eugen Herrigel, which is required reading for the course! Read Harold Clurman's *The Fervent Years* and learn more about the Group Theater and your heritage as an actor. Read *Writing In Restaurants* by David Mamet and *Way of the Peaceful Warrior* by Dan Millman. Read *Timebends*, Arthur Miller's autobiography, *The Empty Space* by Peter Brook, *My Name Is Asher Lev* by Chaim Potok and *The Tao Of Leadership* by John Heider. And, of course, read plays—lots and lots of plays!

A KICK OFF!

Together, we have begun to build the foundation for something of lasting value. True listening, working from your instinct rather than your head, living fully in the moment, your openness and availability to your partners and to yourself, really doing rather than pretending to do and your ability to bring a deep personal meaning to your work. Listen, these skills we have been working on are essential. Without them, acting cannot occur. And, as I said, it is only the beginning.

If we were to continue working together, we would explore other crucial aspects of the craft including: emotional preparation (which is a specific process aimed at making available to you your own deeper truths and allowing access to your rich emotional instrument), tackling the script, the many tools of interpretation, and more advanced ways of bringing a specific and vital life to the characters you play. I would also hope you will be studying voice and diction, movement, dance, and other forms of physical and vocal training. It's a must.

Wrap Up!

I hope you had a powerful rollercoaster ride in doing the exercises and that you are hungry for more! You know, I feel as if you are my extended class and I would love to share in your experiences of the work or to answer any questions you have. Please do not hesitate, I want very badly to hear from you! At the bottom of my biography, you will find all the information in order to contact me.

Be well, my friend.

Love, Larry

Afterword

In the end, this book and the concepts behind it were made for just one thing: to spare the actor from that hollow feeling of fraudulence that we believe comes from not having been able to stimulate in ourselves the emotion appropriate to the task set out for us to do. We berate ourselves, then go on only to look deeper. Meisner knew the trap of that kind of looking, understood that it is like asking of the eye that it study its own retina. "*Il faut s'oublier*," said Duse: "One must forget oneself." In acting, truth can be activated most freely when it is forced to respond to something outside itself. If we can once pay attention to what sits across from us, we free our natures to come up with reactions we could never plan.

Before I began writing for the movies I had longed, as you do, to be an actor. I majored in drama at a university famed for its theatre department. I pounded the pavements on Broadway after the war, auditioning for everything, reading for everyone, even turning down the Theatre Guild because the part they offered seemed too small! It was a time when even a neophyte actor without an agent was welcome to show up at any producer's office in New York. Everyone wanted to help me, but the kinder people were, and the more auditions I went to, the more fraudulent I felt. I realized with shock that my training had not given me anything to rely on except imitation, the elusive inspiration of the moment, and a system for cannibalizing myself. It was nobody's fault: Most teachers then had slight understanding of what Stanislavsky had intended, or of the work being done by the Group Theatre, or of the rebellious young actors just coming out of it to refine their own methods and start their own schools—people like Lee Strasberg, Stella Adler, Sanford Meisner. The teaching given me had come from an age of declamation and theatrical gesture, when you acted the whole play alone in your head and could carry it from town to town like a sample case and give your solo performance no matter what any of the other actors did. The grand stage picture was everything, and the music of the words had to carry—even in a whisper— to the last row of the second balcony. I was lost; I didn't know how people did it, people like Laurette Taylor, and Ethel Waters, and Duse in that tiny scrap of silent film. What made them so real? I thought their acting must come from a special "feeling" they had found, and that if I could catch it once and learn to repeat it at will, I might finally have fuel for the road.

I still have the two gallery shots, on double weight, semigloss paper that I carried on my rounds in New York. There they are, the solemn full-face one and the happy semi-profile one, with the eyebrow arched. I remember perfectly the day I posed for them, straining to capture within my allotted time that "feeling" for each pose that would lift me off a page of the Casting Guide and into the heart of some great producer/mentor. The "feelings" that I worked for in those poses were the same ones I tried to find before every entrance in every role I'd ever tried to play; I believed that if I achieved them, and then clung to them on stage, no matter what was happening around me or what the other actors were doing, I might survive the requisite two hours. Here's what I did to reach the "happy feeling," following the advice of a friend, who by then was also reduced to superstition: I would stand on my tiptoes in the wings as long as I could and tickle the roof of my mouth very fast with the tip of my tongue, while at the same time panting through my nostrils the way antelopes do to cool off. The "solemn feeling" was a combination of memory and anatomy—lashing myself to recall my grief over the death of someone dear, whose face, in the split second before I had to go on, I couldn't even remember. This had to be done while staring as hard as I could at any light shining from the opposite wings and not blinking until my eyes streamed. I also had to tighten my throat until it felt that strangling, yet oddly reassuring sensation of generalized despair that had so often characterized my childhood. Once out on the stage itself, I thought my performance must have been a pleasure to listen to, not only because the *Daily Iowan* said so, but because I was careful to employ my Maurice Evans vibrato for anything Shakespearean, my Eva Le Gallienne voice—with its haunted vowels and rapier consonants—for anything from Chekhov up, and my general-service-Robert-Frost-rural-poet voice for everything American.

I thought I was feeling a lot in those photographs, but looking at them today, all I see is tight self-consciousness and the smiling denial of a desperate appeal for rescue. I hadn't known it then of course because I hadn't met Sanford Meisner, and Larry Silverberg hadn't been born, but by not letting myself be who I was (me), or where I was (in a photographic studio), or with whom I was (the photographer), and by not "taking it all off him," I had insured that everything true about me, everything that might have been interesting, or even alive—had I not striven so hard to put what I thought was "acting" in the way of it—was obliterated. Had I read this artfully simple book then, had there even been such a book (and there is no other now), I would never have had to give up my dream and become a writer.

Forty-five years after those pictures were taken I crept up a terrifying stairway in a Seattle warehouse four times a week all one summer to learn from Larry, in relentless five-hour doses, what you have been learning form this book and from "The Exercise" in all its elaborations. Larry has stuffed himself into his book as if his life depended on it—just as he asks you to do in your activities. He has condensed himself down to the size of a pocket so he can be your portable friend. He has stalked you rudely down the boundaries of your court, correcting your serve and your rally, blowing his whistle at fouls, getting in your face, urging you to keep on doing the work, bit by bit by bit, repeating, repeating without questioning it, taking it from over there, working-off each other, and oh! if you heed him you will recreate yourself in a way you never thought possible, in a way on which you will always be able to rely, in a way that cannot accommodate that hollow feeling of fraudulence, ever again.

There are only two things missing from this workbook: the grace of Larry's waiting as he watches you work, and the deep and liquid darkness of the silences he casts in which he lets you find the answer in yourself. There is a third thing: the chance to sit for an hour at Meisner's feet; Sandy might like that, too. Now go back to page one and start all over again!

—*Stewart Stern*

Loving to Audition

The Audition Workbook for Actors
by Larry Silverberg

"A valuable, adventurous, and enthusiastic entrée into the little defined world of auditioning."

Allan Miller, actor, director, teacher, and author

"Acting coach Larry Silverberg takes two monologues and proceeds for 147 pages to dissect every word, every possible layer of meaning, every possible angle of approach, to show how a master actor would interpret the speeches at an audition. Silverberg supplies so many techniques for climbing inside the brief texts that any actor with the presence of mind to recall a tenth of them in the heat of a real-life audition would have the basis for ample calm confidence. This is a really useful guide for absorbing text quickly — whether for performer or audience."

Drama, Dance, and Theater Editor's
Recommended Book, Amazon.com

includes specific exercises
LOVING TO AUDITION
ISBN 1-57525-007-1, 144 pages, $15.95

Published by Smith and Kraus, Inc.
Available at your local bookstore
or call toll-free (888) 282-2881 www.SmithandKraus.com

The SANFORD MEISNER *Approach*

The best-selling workbook series that opens the door to Meisner's Approach

"Here, Silverberg, who was a student of the master teacher, presents a workbook for actors that will prove useful, regardless of how familiar the reader is with Meisner's methods. Silverberg's writing is concise and insightful throughout and makes the technique accessible to any committed student."
—Library Journal

"For serious theatre students, this book could be highly influential in laying a foundation for their acting careers."
—Voice of Youth Advocates

All books include specific exercises from the Method.

WORKBOOK ONE: AN ACTOR'S WORKBOOK
ISBN 1-880399-77-6, 176 pages, $12.95

WORKBOOK TWO: EMOTIONAL FREEDOM
ISBN 1-57525-074-8, 116 pages, $14.95

WORKBOOK THREE: TACKLING THE TEXT
ISBN 1-57525-130-2, 132 pages, $14.95

WORKBOOK FOUR: PLAYING THE PART
ISBN 1-57525-212-0, 256 pages, $14.95

Published by Smith and Kraus, Inc.
Available at your local bookstore
or call toll-free (888) 282-2881 www.SmithandKraus.com

Smith and Kraus *Books For Actors*

MONOLOGUE SERIES
The Best Men's / Women's Stage Monologues of 1993
The Best Men's / Women's Stage Monologues of 1992
The Best Men's / Women's Stage Monologues of 1991
The Best Men's / Women's Stage Monologues of 1990
One Hundred Men's / Women's Stage Monologues from the 1980's
2 Minutes and Under: Character Monologues for Actors
Street Talk: Character Monologues for Actors
Uptown: Character Monologues for Actors
Monologues from Contemporary Literature: Volume I
Monologues from Classic Plays

FESTIVAL MONOLOGUE SERIES
The Great Monologues from the Humana Festival
The Great Monologues from the EST Marathon
The Great Monologues from the Mark Taper Forum
The Great Monologues from the Women's Project

YOUNG ACTORS SERIES
Great Scenes and Monologues for Children
New Plays from A.C.T.'s Young Conservatory
Great Scenes for Young Actors from the Stage
Great Monologues for Young Actors
Multicultural Monologues for Young Actors
Multicultural Scenes for Young Actors
Villeggiatura: The Trilogy Condensed, Goldoni, tr. by Robert Cornthwaite

SCENE STUDY SERIES
Scenes From Classic Plays 468 B.C. to 1960 A.D.
The Best Stage Scenes of 1993
The Best Stage Scenes of 1992
The Best Stage Scenes for Women from the 1980's
The Best Stage Scenes for Men from the 1980's

CONTEMPORARY PLAYWRIGHTS
Romulus Linney: 17 Short Plays
Eric Overmyer: Collected Plays
Lanford Wilson: 21 Short Plays
William Mastrosimone: Collected Plays
Horton Foote: 4 New Plays
Terrence McNally: 15 Short Plays
Women Playwrights: The Best Plays of 1992
Women Playwrights: The Best Plays of 1993
Humana Festival '93: The Complete Plays
Humana Festival '94: The Complete Plays

GREAT TRANSLATION FOR ACTORS SERIES
The Wood Demon: Anton Chekhov *translated by N. Saunders & F. Dwyer*
The Seagull: Anton Chekhov *translated by N. Saunders & F. Dwyer*
Three Sisters: Anton Chekhov *translated by Lanford Wilson*
Mercadet: Honoré de Balzac *translated by Robert Cornthwaite*

CAREER DEVELOPMENT BOOKS
The Actor's Chekhov
Kiss and Tell: Restoration Scenes, Monologues, & History
Cold Readings: Some Do's and Don'ts for Actors at Auditions
A Shakespearean Actor Prepares
Auditioning For Musical Theater
The Camera Smart Actor

If you require pre-publication information about upcoming Smith and Kraus books, you may receive our catalogue, free of charge, by sending your name and address to *Smith and Kraus Catalogue, P.O. Box 127 One Main Street, Lyme, NH 03768 toll-free (888) 282-2881, fax (603) 643-1831 or www.smithandkraus.com.*

The
Sanford Meisner
Approach

AN ACTOR'S WORKBOOK